THE TENDERHEARTED MOM

The Tenderhearted Mom

Finding Balance Between Gentleness and Toughness

Jan Stoop

SERVANT PUBLICATIONS
ANN ARBOR, MICHIGAN

Vine Books is an imprint of Servant Publications especially designed to serve evangelical Christians.

Published in association with the literary agency of Alive Communications, Inc., 7680 Goddard Street, Suite 200, Colorado Springs, CO 80920.

Unless otherwise indicated, all Scripture quotations are taken from the Holy Bible, New Living Translation, copyright © 1996. Used by permission of Tyndale House Publishers, Inc., Wheaton, Illinois 60189. All rights reserved. Verses marked TLB are from the Living Bible. Verses marked NASB are from the New American Standard Bible.

All testimonies that appear in this book are composites based on the experiences of several people. Names and circumstances have been changed to protect the privacy of individuals who freely shared their stories with the author.

Published by Servant Publications
P.O. Box 8617
Ann Arbor, Michigan 48107

Cover design by Paul Higdon, Minneapolis, Minn.

01 02 03 04 10 9 8 7 6 5 4 3 2 1

Printed in the United States of America
ISBN 1-56955-260-6

Library of Congress Cataloging-in-Publication Data

Stoop, Jan.
    The tenderhearted mom : finding balance between gentleness and toughness / Jan Stoop.
        p. cm.
    Includes bibliographical references.
    ISBN 1-56955-260-6 (alk. paper)
    1. Motherhood—Religious aspects—Christianity.   2. Parenting—Religious aspects—Christianity. I. Title.
    BV4529.18 .S75 2001
    248.8'431—dc21
                                                                                    2001005615

Contents

Foreword

"Do you mind if I steal John for a few minutes?" Jan asked in the midst of a chaotic conference where we were both speakers. "Are you sure about this?" I said in utter relief as she took my rambunctious three-year-old boy by the hand for a little adventure during what was for him a most boring experience. A few minutes later they returned—John proudly carrying a football he had selected from the gift shop at Jan's expense. But what he really sparkled from was her gift of time and attention when he needed it most.

If ever there was a tenderhearted mom—it is Jan. I've seen her extraordinary skills in action as both a mom and grandmother and I've taken notice. Jan's approach to motherhood is like a breath of fresh air to all of us whose personalities lean toward tenderness. It helps us to realize our gifts as moms and to unwrap these gifts, giving generously from our heart. But is also brings to bear the wisdom of a mom who can teach us well how to "strengthen our week knees" in the area of toughness meeting the inevitable challenges of bringing up children of character and strength.

I encourage you to study this book enthusiastically. I am confident it will find a place of importance in your home—as it has in mine—where it sits with a small collection of well-worn and much-used parenting resources.

Leslie Parrott

Prologue

As I sat one night thinking about how I might explain better the integrated balance of tender and tough called for in how we love our kids, I was surprised to see, out of the corner of my eye, movement in the next room. A bird! How had this beautiful tiny creature gotten into the house anyway? Had he come in during the day and had somehow been quiet enough that I did not notice him? We had never had a bird come in at night. Just then this little trapped bird began a furious flight pattern. For the next hour he flew from the top of the shutters in the living room to the top of the lampshade, and then on to the kitchen shelf and then to the shutters in the family room where I sat. Back and forth he flew, at times bumping into the wall as he desperately tried to find his way out.

This night I did not have time to deal with, of all things, a bird. I had determined not to answer the phone and not to get distracted by the millions of things I could see in my house that needed my attention. I was going to really focus on the writing that needed to be done. But alas, it was just not going to happen. I got up. I thought if I opened every door and window, that maybe, just maybe the problem would take care of itself. Then I thought that if I turned out all the lights and turned on the outside lights that surely he would see where the openings were. But no, this little bird could not see that he was making terrible decisions. He blindly overlooked the open doors and windows and continued to beat himself up trying again and again to get out by flying at shutters and windows that could not be opened.

As I watched, I was drawn in more and more by the futility of his efforts. I really felt for him. At times I followed him from room to room, thinking that maybe he would stay still long enough for me to throw a shirt over him, making it possible for me to rescue him. But he sensed that I was following him and it made him all the more desperate. I frantically searched for our homemade net that we had used to rescue other birds in the past. It was not in the closet where it was usually kept. I watched helplessly. I tried to sit down and get to my work. But I could not. This suffering little creature was my focus.

Finally, I heard futile fluttering, as the bird got himself caught behind the plants that I have sitting in front of the window in the kitchen. He was tired. He probably thought he was going to die. He did not know that I was going to be tender with him. Gently I threw the shirt I had been carrying over his frantic little body. He lay still. *Did he die*, I wondered. *Did I kill him?* He was so still. *What to do now?* I very gently, and, as tenderly as I could, scooched the shirt under him and lifted up the little bundle. I couldn't tell if he was even in the shirt—he was so little and so light. Then I saw a little wing poke out from the fold in the shirt. What compassion I felt for this little one. Somehow I wanted him to know that I was not trying to hurt him further, but that I was trying to be as tender as I could possibly be, and that I wanted to set him free. As I took him outside, I gingerly opened the fold of the shirt. He hesitated a moment, then he took off into the night—looking as if he would be OK.

My evening was spent, and I was a bit angered at the seemingly wasted time. But as I began to let my mind settle a bit, I was suddenly struck with the fact that God had just allowed me, in some small way, to experience a model of his tenderness and toughness, just what I had been trying to write about! I think he wanted me to see that the tenderness I felt toward that little bird was somehow integrated with the toughness required to capture it and set it free. The evening wasn't wasted—God graciously gave me a clear picture of the love he has for us and the love that he intends us to have for our children—love that is tender, gentle, and compassionate, yet also tough.

Part One

The Tenderhearted Mom's Dilemma

Chapter One

The Gift of the Tender Heart

*The loveliest masterpiece of the heart of God
is the heart of a mother.*

THÉRÈSE OF LISIEUX

"So, Mom, what are you gonna write about?" one of my sons asked, after I had told my family that I was going to start another writing project.

We were all standing around in my small kitchen, watching this son cook for a family birthday dinner—he is the cook in the family and we all enjoy letting him do it.

"Well, it's going to be something about moms who are tenderhearted," I hedged, thinking that would be the end of it.

"And what are you going to say about them?" another son, Greg, asked with a knowing smile.

I hesitantly went on, as I really didn't want their advice on the subject—I wasn't ready to risk having my mothering skills brought up for discussion. "You know," I said, "about how a mom might be so tenderhearted and love her kids so much, that she has trouble ..."

Then one of the kids jumped in and said, "I can remember once when you were really tough with me."

"Once?" I incredulously replied. I had heard this story before but I always took the bait.

15

"You remember," he went on, "it was when I asked if I could buy a motorcycle, and you and Dad both said, absolutely not! So see, one time you did say 'no,'" he said jokingly.

I somewhat impatiently listened and then began to feel that I needed to defend myself. "But you do remember how strict I was when you were little, don't you? Don't you remember all the 'no's' I said back then?" I asked.

All three of my grown sons have a wonderful, and yet sometimes irritating, teasing-type sense of humor that obviously comes from my Irish husband's side of the family. It sure doesn't come from mine—we enjoy funny stuff but don't tease like his family. As the only female in the household (except for our female pets) until our sons married, I have borne the brunt of their humor since day one. It gives me great sympathy for the daughters-in-law who have married into our family. Much of what my sons have teased me about seems somehow to be connected to how tenderhearted I am. They don't use that term but they rail on how I spoil the dog, and the grandchildren, how I rescue people, birds, and animals, and how I worry about babies I hear crying in restaurants, and on and on it goes. They know what a "softie" I am.

You see, I am a tenderhearted mom and I know that in many situations I have not been tough enough as a mother. Thankfully, all three sons have survived my tender style of mothering, but I wish I had realized earlier that stronger, more definite limits would have been to their benefit, and mine. I have come to realize that there were many times when I needed a tougher, more objective attitude, especially in situations that came up as my children grew into their teen years. It may have helped prevent some of the deep painful times that we faced.

I meet and talk to many moms who struggle with how to balance their tenderness with the toughness needed in mothering. And many of them have felt frustrated, as I have, with much of the "helpful" advice that tells a mom to get tough but seems to negate the true power of the tender heart. Some fail to recognize the tender heart as an incredible gift from our Heavenly Father.

Yes, we moms need to get tough! But there are some things we tenderhearted moms have to understand.

Toughness has to be more than an act. Learning to act tough in certain situations is extremely helpful as we will see as we look at the principles of "tough love." But there's more to it. We tenderhearted moms must understand that setting limits comes out of the love and strength that a tender heart can give. True toughness comes *because* we have a tender heart, not in spite of it.

In talking to moms who described themselves as tenderhearted, I found that every one of them wanted to be, and they were all trying to be, the best mother they could possibly be. But the majority of them spoke of their struggle to integrate just the right amount of toughness into their tenderness. They wanted their kids to experience both love and limits. They asked questions like, "Is it OK that I care so deeply about everything and everybody, especially my kids? Will it ruin their lives if I don't get tough enough? Does that make me codependent? What if I'm just naturally more tenderhearted? Will I have to change my personality?" One mom said, "I try to get tough, but my kids still pay no attention until I get really mad and then I react in anger. Then I get really tough, but I don't like what I see in myself when that happens. I know that that's not the right way to set limits but I can't seem to do it any other way." Another mom asked, "How can I learn to set limits when so much advice available seems to make me feel inadequate and put down? What will I be like if I become tough? Will my family still love me?" These moms wanted to have some answers that would see them through all the years of parenting, not just get them through a crisis.

These questions and others that I hear moms ask, have helped motivate me to share what has helped me in my struggle to be both tender and tough. We will look at the roots of tenderness to see why a mom leans to being sometimes "too tender" and why she may unhealthily hang on to her identity as the soft and tender woman, often to the exclusion of any place for toughness. We will also look at how some efforts to resolve the dilemma can be fruitless and other efforts extremely healing and life changing. We will look at the tender heart as a God-given gift. We'll see that when we begin to appreciate it as a gift, we are then able to understand how God chooses to use our tenderness to our advantage. He can use it to give us strength and confidence to get tough when it's called for. And he wants to use it to create tender spirits in our kids.

The Gift of Tenderness

Once at a meeting where I was to speak to young mothers, a woman sitting in the back asked me what I was going to talk about. When I said that the topic was going to be about tenderness and toughness, she said, "Oh, you should meet my husband

and hear what he says about tenderness." *I thought, how interesting. It's usually the women who want to talk about tenderness, not the men.* She went on to tell me his story. She said that her husband remembers that his mom had treated him with tenderness throughout his childhood. His mom had not only treated all her children with tenderness, but she had taught them the value of tenderness in all relationships by often speaking to them about what she called "gentle hands." His mom taught him and his siblings that treatment with gentle hands created gentle spirits. She went on to tell me that now that her husband's mom is elderly and in a nursing home, her husband goes to visit her every day. Her husband tells her, "I learned tenderness through the 'gentle hands' of my mom, and it was not lost on me. Now I want to make sure that her gift of 'gentle hands' is passed back to her. It is my privilege to go sit with her and pat her hand, plump her pillow and smooth out her blankets. I tell her I love her and at mealtimes I try to coax her to eat by using the same little games she used with me. Sometimes she doesn't respond to me, but I know that she senses that I am there. It's the gift of tenderness that I am giving back to her." What a wonderful son and husband he must be!

Tenderness is a necessary ingredient for life. Babies thrive when they receive it and die when deprived of it. It shouldn't surprise us that children of all ages, teenagers, and adults need tenderness all throughout life, too, as it characterizes the connection underlying loving human relationships. We all not only need tender, gentle treatment and blossom when we get it, but we also desire it in such intensity that we will go to great lengths to be with a person who gives it to us.

The descriptive word "tender" is defined in *Webster's College Dictionary*[1] as "soft or delicate in substance, not hard or tough; delicate or gentle and kind; easily moved to sympathy or compassion; affectionate or sentimental." The human quality of tenderness speaks of all this and more. To be tender means that we are lovingly responsive to others, making ourselves available and accessible to others when they need us and accepting them without judgment. It is intertwined in the concept of love, and yet tenderness has a meaning of its own. Tenderness in humans can be found everywhere, that is, if one is looking for it. We see tenderness in a little girl who so gently and carefully picks up her new little kitten. It is felt in a mother's note found in a child's lunch box that says, "I love you." It is in the warm hug given to a friend whose heart is breaking over a recent loss. It is in a father's comfort as he whispers in the ear of his fearful child during a thunderstorm, "It's OK, you are safe. I am here with you."

Tenderness is a gift of love that can be conveyed by a touch, a look, words, or even an attitude, and every one of us who shows tenderness to another person gives it a new facet of meaning. By giving it, we are able to mirror to others in some way the tenderness that God shows to us.

What Does It Mean to Be "Tenderhearted"?

When we put the words "tender" and "heart" together, the meaning of both words intensifies. We all use the word *heart* in our everyday conversations. Sometimes, because it is so commonly used, we don't stop to think what we really mean. We say, "Let's get to the heart of the matter," "He didn't have the heart for it," or "She really broke his heart." Song titles and book titles abound that contain the word *heart*. Songs like "You Gotta Have Heart" or "I Left My Heart in San Francisco" attempt to describe the depth of our feelings. In fact, I recently learned that book titles and song titles containing the word *heart* outsell others, probably because we are drawn to the word that signifies so deep a part of us.

There are many definitions that can be applied to *heart*, and they can help us understand how we have struggled over the centuries to understand the heart. Here are just a few from the *Webster's College Dictionary:*

- The center of the personality, especially with reference to intuition, feeling, or emotion; as "in your heart you know it's true."
- The center of emotion, especially as contrasted to the head as the center of the intellect.
- Capacity for sympathy; feeling; affection; as in, "his heart moved him to help the needy."
- Spirit, courage, or enthusiasm; as in "to lose heart."
- The innermost or central part of anything; as in "the heart of Paris."
- The vital or essential part; core; as in "the heart of the matter."
- Core; a strand running through the center of a rope, the other strands being laid around it.

So when we speak of a tender heart, we refer to that center of us wherein resides that ability to show tenderness in the form of gentleness, mercy, compassion, and kindness.

Tenderheartedness is a trait that is highly valued in anyone, male or female, and it flows from the heart of the very One who so tenderly made us in his image—our heavenly Father.

The Tender Heart of God

Many biblical passages refer to the tenderness of God. We get a picture of his tender heart throughout the Scriptures as we read of the tenderness that he shows in his availability, responsiveness, and acceptance as he deals with those he loves. For example, the psalmist wrote, "I love the Lord because he hears and answers my prayers. Because he bends down and listens, I will pray as long as I have breath!" (Ps 116:1). Do you get a sense of how tenderhearted God is if he cares for us enough to bend down to listen to us?

We as God's children are somewhat like the little child who was straining to hear what a very tall man was saying to her. The little girl stood on her tippy-toes and looked up at the man and said, "Will you please come down here so that we can talk?" The man was taken aback. After a moment's hesitation, he knelt down on his knees and looked her in the eyes. The little girl said, "That's better. I can talk to you now." God so tenderly loves us that he wants to meet us where we are so that he can hear us.

In Zephaniah 3:17 we are told that God even sings over us. What a wonderfully tender behavior! "For the Lord your God has arrived to live among you. He is a mighty savior. He will rejoice over you with great gladness. With his love, he will calm all your fears. He will exult over you by singing a happy song."

Some of the most precious times I have had with my children and now have with my grandchildren, are the times when I rock them and sing over them. What wonderful closeness I feel as I cuddle them and sing songs like, "There Is Power in the Blood of the Lamb." I know that they do not understand the words, but somewhere deep down I know they feel the power of those words. Their fears are calmed as they snuggle up on my lap and I know that they tuck these experiences away deep down inside of them, memories that they will be able to draw upon later. To think that God loves me so much that he sings over me, tells me a lot about his tenderheartedness. (In a later chapter, we will look more in depth at those images of God we find in Scripture that show him as tenderhearted.)

Not only are we lifted and encouraged by reading of God's tenderheartedness, but we are also encouraged to develop our own tender hearts as we become more like Christ. Clearly, tenderheartedness is a virtue spoken of throughout Scripture, a positive quality that we can all manifest. Here are two passages that challenge us to have a tender heart.

"Finally, all of you should be of one mind, full of sympathy toward each other, loving one another with tender hearts and humble minds" (1 Pt 3:8).

"Since God chose you to be the holy people whom he loves, you must clothe yourselves with tenderhearted mercy, kindness, humility, gentleness, and patience" (Col 3:12).

He wants us to have a tender heart that closely imitates his own heart, and he knows that mothers, especially, need to have a capacity for expressing his kind of tenderness.

Moms and Tenderness

Motherhood probably has the highest regard our culture can give. When I hear an athlete say to the TV camera, "Hi, Mom!" I think, *Oh, how nice it is that he's thinking of his mom*. He's honoring her and is, in some way, trying to acknowledge the important part that she's played in where he is today. We often praise our moms, and when we think of them, what most often comes to mind is their compassion and tenderness. In 1914, a presidential proclamation exhorted our entire country to set aside an official day in honor of mothers, declaring the second Sunday of May to be a day of celebration of mothers. Anna Jarvis, an unmarried schoolteacher, pressed her idea about having a day to honor mothers to government officials until they took her seriously. She wanted to honor the memory of her own mom whom she had cared for fifteen years until her death in 1905. If the proclamation Anna Jarvis so tirelessly fought for had listed the qualities she wanted us to honor in mothers, I'm quite sure the list would have included a tender heart.

Over the centuries, warm thoughts concerning motherhood and a mother's qualities have probably been written about as frequently as thoughts about most any other subject. Consider what these three historical figures said about their moms:

Mark Twain: "My mother had a slender, small body, but a large heart—a heart so large that everybody's grief and everybody's joys found welcome in it, and hospitable accommodation."

John Quincy Adams: "My mother was an angel upon earth. She was a minister of blessing to all with her tender spirit.... She had no feelings but of kindness and gentleness."

Alfred Lord Tennyson: "My mother was as mild as any saint ... so gracious was her tact and tenderness."

It's obvious that these men held their tenderhearted moms in the highest regard.

Most of our sentiments about motherhood capture aspects that show our mothers to be the center of our lives and the givers of gentleness and tenderness. Children tell of the love and tenderness that they feel from Mom, too. Here are a few thoughts kids shared when asked how they knew their moms loved them:

Tara, age 6: "After school my mom tells me to go get my special blanket and then we cuddle up in our big chair and we talk about my day. I love it when we do that."

Scottie, age 5: "My mom gets a little mad when I ask her for things while she's on the phone. But she hurries and she doesn't stay mad very long because she loves me so much."

Brittany, age 7: "My mom is gentle and kind and holds me when I get hurt. She also plays dolls with me when I can't have a friend over, and lets the cat sleep on my bed when I am sick."

Chelsea, age 9: "I know my mom loves me because she is gentle and she always stands up for me, no matter what. And she never lectures me in a mad way."

My own little six-year-old grandson, David, said, "Mom tells me that she loves me 'up to the moon and back' every time I get out of the car at school!"

Colleen, my ten-year-old granddaughter, put on her mom's birthday card, "What I love best about you is that you are full of joy and I know you love me because you ask me to forgive you when you do something wrong."

Do you sense the warmth that is reflected in these children's views of their moms? They seem to agree that they know their moms love them and they obviously value the way in which she shows her love. Moms do often show certain qualities that allow them to demonstrate their love in very tender ways. In fact, most of us value in her that very special quality more than any other virtue that a mother possesses.

A few weeks ago, while shopping at a large department store in downtown Cincinnati, where my husband and I were to speak at a conference, I became so fascinated by a mom who exhibited such tenderness that I couldn't help stopping to observe. I was looking for some warm socks to stave off the drafty chill that seemed to hover over the floor in the hotel meeting room. I had forgotten how cold it could get in that part of the country, even in the early fall. I couldn't resist taking a quick look at the coats, too, when I noticed that this store had a much larger selection than our stores at home in California.

As I wandered through the coat department, I heard a woman's lilting voice from another aisle saying, "Peek-a-boo, I see you. Do I know your mother? Yes, I do! Where is that mother of yours? Oh, here she is. She sees you!" And then, "I love you!" On and on this one-sided conversation went. I couldn't see around all the garment racks, and I was getting curious. The voice was obviously that of a mom talking to her little one. When I peered around the racks of coats into the next aisle, I expected to see a tired, bored toddler sitting in a stroller and his mom trying to keep him distracted as she shopped. How surprised I was to see that this mom had been talking to a very tiny baby, probably only a few weeks old. I was awestruck.

I wondered if she knew how important it is for even the youngest baby to hear his mom's voice. I thought what an excellent mom she must be! I sensed the warmth in her words and the reassuring sound of her voice. How comforting that must have been to her infant! As I watched, every few minutes, she reached down to gently pat her little one who was wrapped snugly in his blanket. She seemed to be assuring him with her voice and touch that his mom was right there close beside him. I was impressed by her tenderness and the sense of security she was implanting within that tiny little life.

I'm always drawn in by the tenderness I see displayed by moms wherever I go. And when it's right under my nose, in my own family, I feel especially privileged to see it. As a mother of three sons, I don't have daughters of my own, but I have been blessed with tenderhearted daughters-in-law. (I hasten to add that I see it in my sons, too, as they have turned out to be very tenderhearted fathers). Time after time, God allows me to see those special moments that are evidence of the deeply felt tenderness a mother can give. When I see Pati patiently hold little three-year-old Jonathan to give him the extra time he needs to fully wake up, or see Terri's tenderness as she listens compassionately to ten-year-old Colleen tell of a painful disappointment, I see tenderness in both of them that amazes even this tenderhearted grandma. I know that these little ones are being impacted for life by the tenderness and gentleness they are receiving from their mothers. A mom's tender treatment builds a reservoir of love deep within her children, a source from which they can draw as they form their perception of themselves and their world. It will last them all their lives.

Our adult children thrive on appropriate doses of a mom's tenderness, too. Recently one of my daughters-in-law called me on the phone and said, "Hey! We all need a mom up here to give us some mothering!" Both kids and parents were fighting a flu bug and they had come to the end of their rope. Of course I was delighted to respond, and I knew that she was asking me to show them some tender loving care. Sometimes we forget that the need for tenderness does not end when our children reach adulthood. In a world that is harsh and cold, many times tenderness is the powerful sustenance that gives an adult child the confidence to make it through tough times.

A mom's tenderness not only leaves a permanent imprint on her children as it "fills them up," but it is so powerful that it changes her as the mom, too.

The Power of Tenderness

It's a bit scary to jump into something knowing that there's no turning back. Becoming a mother is like that. Once you've become a mom, that's it. Not only is your lifestyle turned upside down; the way you love is forever changed, too. Nothing will ever be quite the same again. Something powerful has been activated deep down inside—some dimension of tenderness that lies dormant in a woman until that day when she gives birth.

In her book, *The Power of Mother Love*, Dr. Brenda Hunter speaks of the powerful effect motherhood has on us:

Ah, the power of mother love. How it stretches and swells across generations, uniting mother and child, fleshing out the expectant mother's identity and femininity, shaping the personality and life of her child, and changing society in ways our culture has chosen to ignore. Mother love is ultimately a love song, a siren's call, luring women to new ways of being ... to sacrifice and being turned inside out ... to fulfillment. Mother love transforms a woman, forever changing the way she defines herself.[2]

I can remember so clearly the day I brought my first baby home from the hospital. There in that little New York community, on a beautiful, cool October day, my husband, Dave, and I so carefully and awkwardly got our little bundled-up baby out of the car and carried him to the side door entrance that led to our tiny upstairs apartment. We quietly crept through the kitchen of the owners' quarters, the only way to get to the stairs that led to our tiny living space. Dave was a college student, and we were thankful to have that little place to ourselves, a home to which we could bring our first baby. Here we made our first attempts at being a "real" family.

I remember carefully removing the little receiving blanket that was barely large enough to cover our baby's nine pounds and thinking what an awesome thing it was to have this helpless, totally dependent little creature in our hands. And I also remember thinking scary thoughts like, *I am into this forever! Am I adequate for this? Can I handle it? Who will tell me what to do?* With no family or close friends around to give advice and support, my husband and I were thrown into those scary waters of parenthood that felt totally uncharted and uncertain to us.

That first day we sat down and took stock of what we knew about caring for a baby. Oh, we knew that you must always support his head when holding him, and about diapering and a little about nursing and burping, but not much else. Certainly, we didn't know the importance of his very first relationship—the attachment that our little one was forming in his first days with Mom and Dad, and how much he was learning about his world just from the treatment we were giving him. But what I was least prepared for were the changes that took place deep inside of me, changes in my heart.

I knew that somehow, someway, I wanted to give this child all that I could to help him thrive in this world. I didn't know exactly how I would do that, so I did what I knew best to do. I gave him my love and treated him with tenderness. As I did, I became very aware of, and somewhat surprised at, something that was being touched and changed deep inside me. A new tender part of my heart was being tapped. As I gave tender love, more welled up inside of me. I somehow knew that from that point on, a part of my heart would be forever walking around outside of me. It would be the investment I would make into my child's life.

Tenderness invades our lives in a quiet, but powerful, way. Whether we receive tenderness, or give it, it changes us. It changes those we give it to as it helps nurture a tender spirit in them. And whom do we want to have a tender spirit more than our own children? If we as moms can recognize and then experience the strength that comes from the tender heart, we will be much better prepared to meet the challenges that parenting surely brings. How will we do that? What follows are the things I have discovered in my mothering journey that have helped me in my own struggle to learn how to appreciate and trust my own tender heart.

A Look Ahead

In this chapter we have looked at the tender heart as a gift from God. I have found that it is *because* of our God-given tender heart, not in spite of it, that we gain the strength to be the mothers we were meant to be. We don't have to rid ourselves of tenderness—it's not something that needs to be "fixed" in us. Instead, we can to learn how to set limits, and do the tough things, *in the context of our tenderness.* A large part of the process is to find the balance of enough tenderness and enough toughness that works right for us. We can listen and take in the advice of many, but ultimately it comes down to what is best for us and our relationship with our child, whether that child is three months old, three years old, or a thirty-three-year-old adult.

In the chapters that follow, we will look at the importance of setting limits, at the concept of "tough love," and at the different attempts that those seeking tender-tough balance have tried. In looking at those attempts, many of us wonder about the factor of personality and what it may have to do with how tender we are and how we learn to set limits and get tough. We will see how our own personality bent and the individual temperament of each of our children affects how we work out the tender-tough issues. Often we take for granted the nature of our child, thinking that treating all children the same will bring the same outcomes.

We will also look at how our past affects our present mothering styles. Often we underestimate the influence of how we were mothered and how it contributes to who we are and to the complexity of tender-tough issues in our own efforts at mothering. Of the many factors that contribute to how we mother our children, our own first relationship—the one that we formed with our own moms—has the greatest and most powerful influence. We will consider three basic needs we had as children and look at how we were "filled up" when they were met, and left with empty "cups" when they were not. Looking at the kind of attachment we formed with our moms can provide us with very important clues as to how to balance gentleness and toughness in our relationships with our children.

Next we will look at the plan God has for healing past hurts in tenderhearted moms. I believe God allows things to come into our paths to say, "Look here. Pay attention. I have a better way." He has many ways to help us become aware of areas in our lives that need his healing touch, and he often uses disturbances in relationships—usually relationships to our husbands and children—to show us what he wants to heal. Many times those disturbances point to wounds that may have come as a result of faulty relationships in childhood. We get stuck with inaccurate views of ourselves and of those close to us and consequently get stuck in unhealthy patterns of relating, until we learn how God wants to set us free of them. Those patterns usually involve the tender-tough issue. In God's plan, there is a better way.

Finally, we will look at the practicalities of meeting the challenge of what our kids need from us. For that is the purpose in looking at our own mothering history—so that we may begin to understand how we can love our children enough to get tough, and stay tender enough that they have a chance to develop gentle spirits because of our "gentle hands."

Thoughts to Consider:
The tender heart is God's gift to us, a gift that imitates his own tender heart. Tenderness is powerful in that it changes me when I receive it and changes those I treat with tenderness, creating in them a tender spirit and a reservoir of love that will be with them for life.

Can you think of an act of tenderness that you received that made a lasting impression on you? How did it change something in you?

Have you ever received a message that suggested that to be tender is a weakness and not a strength?

How have you experienced your tender heart to be a strength?

A Mom's Prayer

Dear Heavenly Father,

Will you help me to better understand your character and help me to see you as the tenderhearted God that you are? Thank you for loving me so much that you will even bend down toward me in order to hear my prayers. I want to appreciate the tender heart that you placed in me and yet sometimes I have trouble seeing it as strength. I sometimes doubt that I am adequate for the challenges of mothering, and I often wonder if my own tender heart gets in the way. Help me to see that you gave it to me for a purpose. And will you help me to give the "gentle hands" message clearly to my children, by reminding me to treat them in ways that will nurture a tender spirit in them and prepare them to receive your tender love?

In the name of your Son, Jesus,
Amen

Chapter Two

But Love Requires Toughness, Too

Limits are the earth under a child's feet,
a wall against which they can feel
the contours of themselves.

ALEXANDRA STODDARD

I only met her once, but I was in awe of her tough exterior. She was a major in the U.S. Air Force serving at the base where my husband, Dave, and I were leading a seminar. We'd been invited to speak to a squadron of fighter pilots who were having some difficulties getting along with each other when they weren't flying. We were asked to teach team-building skills, how to recognize differences in teammates' personalities, and how to learn to appreciate those differences.

The major was a trainer with many years of experience dealing with young officers and recruits. And for some reason, she had chosen to sit in on our workshop. After the seminar, she came up to me and said, "Don't you think that any one of us could just learn to act or be the way we want to be?" Then without waiting for an answer, she continued, "Take me, for example. Everyone around here knows I am pretty tough. But I had to learn to be tough. I don't think it was my natural bent. But now no one gets away with anything when I'm around. Most of my colleagues aren't like me. They come across as wimps.

And then they whine about the lack of respect they get. We're military, for goodness' sake! I believe anyone can learn to be tough. I'm the first to admit it takes hard work, but these guys don't even try!"

Then she made a remarkable claim: "Just give me enough time with any one of these soft, sensitive officers and I'll make him into 'one tough cookie'—and when I'm finished, he'll thank me for it!"

I've thought a lot about what the major said. *Is it possible to "toughen up" a tender heart? Could she really do as she said and drill the tenderness out and make someone be tough? I wondered what she would do with me if I were her student? And after her program, would I then be better able to respond to the needs of my kids by being tough?*

Mothering: Tough Work for the Tenderhearted

No one said it was going to be easy, this business of being a mom. But most of the moms I have talked to have expressed surprise at the complexities involved in mothering. We love being moms, and none of us would exchange the experience for anything in the world. Many of us have found that along with the incredible joys that motherhood brings also come the trials—periods of time when we think we will not survive with our hearts intact, times when our tender hearts get broken. It's the challenge of motherhood, to be able to weather the storms, somehow keeping mother and child intact through it all. It's difficult for tenderhearted moms. Listen to some tenderhearted moms as they tell of their painful experiences in mothering.

One new mom approached me after a meeting at a Christian camp and tearfully told me her story. She said that she and her husband had been given a book about how to raise kids as a baby shower gift. They had just had their first baby. She told me of the terrible pain she was feeling as her husband insisted on following the book's advice precisely and that he would not let her go pick up their two-week-old son when he cried. She said that her heart was being ripped apart as she felt intensely that she was right and that she needed and wanted to respond to her baby's cries and to hold him and cuddle him. But she also wanted to do it "right," and wondered how she could reconcile what was going on inside of her with what the book advised. (I quickly said to this mom, throw out the book, run to that little one and give him every bit of tender love you can muster!)

A mom of a troubled teenager said that she was being torn apart inside trying to decide whether or not to stick to the boundary she had set about not letting her seventeen-year-old daughter come around the house. Her daughter had been using drugs, but had now been clean for several months, and was asking if she could move back home. This mom, who was single and raising two younger children, expressed great fear that if she let her older daughter come back, even knowing that she was not now using drugs, she would be a bad influence on the other kids. This mom said that it was the worst scenario she could have ever imagined facing, trying to make a choice that might hurt one or the other of her children. What was this mom to do?

Another mom said that she felt confused about what to do when her thirty-three-year-old son kept asking her for money.

He had been on his own for several years, but now he was divorced and having a really hard time emotionally and financially. She felt she had given as much as she could. But how hard it was, she said, to see him in so much pain and not help him out in some way. She wanted to at least help with his kids. She couldn't imagine giving them up to a day-care situation. She had been babysitting them on and off for the last two years and wondered if in getting tough, did it mean that she would not be able to baby-sit at all? Was taking care of his kids enabling him, keeping him from making it on his own?

The mom of a toddler and a six-month-old baby said that she felt that her life was totally out of control. She became overwhelmed when she had a second child and said that she had given up on trying to keep order. Lately, her two-year-old had been really acting up and she said that she could tell that he needed some structure and more time with her, yet she had found she was not able to provide either. "It's very painful," she said, "to love your kids so much and determine each morning that you are going to take the time to enjoy them, but then you find you get so frustrated with them that you end up yelling at them instead. I wonder what is wrong with me. I wish someone could come in and help relieve some of the pressure I feel so that I could have a chance to find myself again. I want my kids to know me as the tender, loving person that I really am, not an angry ogre." With none of her extended family living close enough to help and without a lot of support from her husband, this mom felt alone and overwhelmed. She was at a loss as to how to get back to her tender self to set appropriate limits without waiting until she was so frustrated that she reacted in anger.

It may be that your own situation is not as intense or as desperate as what these moms face, or maybe you identify perfectly with what they are feeling. But all tenderhearted moms struggle with how to be tough in situations that call for it. We want to know how strong our "no's" are to be, what limits are appropriate, and when to stand strong with a boundary.

Moms who care immensely about their children all want to do it "right." They want to be "good enough" moms. But sometimes things don't go as planned. Many moms have found, just as I did, that they are at times called on to give something other than what they've thought they were the best at giving, or to decide things that called for wisdom they did not feel they had. They are faced with the tender-tough dilemma.

With all the advice available to moms, you would think that we could depend on finding good answers to the dilemma to help us get through the problem times. However, I have found that giving advice is easy. Being a real mom is hard. Sometimes moms say they've felt criticized by those who've told them they just weren't tough enough. Sometimes they've tried to act tougher than they've felt, and it has worked—at least for a while. But moms need better answers that can give them strength for the long haul.

The Elusive Balance

We cannot do it perfectly—no mom ever has. But children do need both tenderness and toughness. Tenderhearted moms have the capacity to express tenderness in most cases, but some need help and healing so that they can be the avenue for God's tenderness balanced with toughness to flow through them to their children. So how do we find the balance so that our kids will get what they need?

One mom who shared her story with me amusingly said that as she tried to be the tougher mother she thought she should be, she sometimes compared herself to Goldilocks in the story of the Three Bears. Heeding advice, she said she tried out the "hard stuff" of being tougher, and found it didn't feel quite right and that it was a little "too hard." Then she quickly retreated back to the "soft stuff" of being more tender. At least that felt more familiar even if she knew it was a little "too soft." She said it wasn't until she faced some serious problems with her kids that she found how much tender and how much tough was "just right" for her.

My experience has been similar. I have found that many moms don't find the right balance until later in the game, many times only after they come up against a serious and painful situation. It's in the face of that painful situation that we all of a sudden want a crash course in setting the boundaries that are needed. Moms tell me that they wish that they could have found out earlier, before a crisis, what it was that might have helped them find the balance between being gentle enough and tough enough in their mothering style.

In recent years all kinds of ideas about how to deal with the tender-tough issues have surfaced. Most moms have been exposed to and embrace the idea that love without limits is not good either for them or for their children. But they are still not able to put into practice the balance that they know is best.

We may seek help. But outside help for situations that have begun to feel out of control may seem to muddy the water further if that help does not include a consideration of the deeper issues of how we got to be the kind of mother we are. Help that provides guidance in the sometimes painful task of shedding any faulty expectations we have about ourselves is critical. But the long way around is more difficult. Most of us still would prefer a quicker answer. Maybe getting a tutor like the Air Force major to teach us "tough" would be the way to go.

Let's take a look at the frequently misunderstood (or misused) approaches to the issues of tenderness and toughness. I see three different models that emerge in the attempt to get "tough."

Our Attempts to Balance Tender With Tough

The "Militaristic" Model

The first approach I refer to as the militaristic model, because, indeed it can feel militaristic and regimented. It is an aggressive way to develop toughness. It is the approach of the major we met earlier. It says, wipe out who you are and become someone else by sheer willpower. Some counselors advocate a very assertive approach to compensate for being too tender. The tender heart is considered to be the problem, something that needs to be changed, or replaced with a better, tougher attitude.

This "militaristic" approach can make a too-tender mom feel like she is inadequate and that she must try to become a totally different person in order to provide what her child needs. Her temperament, her tenderness, is somehow now wrong. Her style of mothering that she thought drew upon her very best traits is not valued. Like me, she might ask if it could be that the very thing that she thought was a God-given gift, the thing she thought she was best at, was actually the very thing that was the problem. In this model, stiff training seems to be what is needed, so tutors like the major might be in great demand.

This approach represents an either-or type of thinking. Many tenderhearted moms are also plagued with perfectionistic tendencies. If a mom is already thinking in either-or terms, a symptom of perfectionism, she may find in this approach the fitting idea that one is either tough or tender, not both together. One gives up tender to be tough, or gives up tough to get tender again.

And in the perfectionist's search for doing it "right," a perfectionistic mom may feel that just trying harder will do it. She doesn't believe the adage, "trying harder will get you more of the same." She thinks that if she can just learn more about it and try harder, surely she will get it perfect.

But in using either of these thinking systems, moms often fail in the attempt to get tough and end up deeply disappointed and blame themselves. Depression may be the result. An approach that gives room for tenderness and toughness to stand side by side is healthier and works out much better.

The Recovery Tough Love Model

When my husband and I faced a desperate situation in our family, we joined a family recovery group made up of families who were in crisis because of drugs or alcohol. There in that group and in the many to follow, we both hammered out our ideas about "tough love," or should I say they were hammered into us.

With today's emphasis and study in the area of setting personal boundaries with "tough love," many counselors, programs, and books use what I call the recovery model. It is definitely a step forward from the militaristic model. I can testify that using tough love works in appropriate situations.

Tough love typically means that one party sets a limit or boundary on what he or she will allow in a relationship by giving a two-part message. It goes something like, "I love you and want you in my life, but I will not and cannot put up with what you are doing. If you continue to do what you are doing, then (fill in the consequences)." Tough love sends the message of tough simultaneously with the message of love, with the recipient hopefully getting both messages. The dissonance of the two messages is framed to get the attention of the one who is acting out, making him or her become aware of the consequences of their actions.

In dealing with marriage problems, tough love can be extremely effective. It involves the necessity for a healthy dose of tough love for marriages in trouble. For example, in a marriage in which one partner has been unfaithful, the other partner has to set a boundary, saying, I will not allow this in my life anymore. Indeed, marriages have been turned around when one partner, in most cases the wife, found that she had power to set limits on what she would allow in her marriage relationship. Not much direction is provided by the tough love approach, however, about how she can get back to a place of tenderness if her wandering spouse repents.

Tough love principles have also been advocated for parents of teens and adult children. And again, there have been some miraculous turnarounds. Tough love principles designed to stop painful behavior can have strong effects on both parent and child, whether that child is a teenager or an adult. One has to start somewhere. Sometimes it takes a little teeth gritting, jumping in, and taking a stand in regard to a particular behavior in order to get the message across about the consequences of crossing boundaries. These emergency procedures can be very effective when used properly.

But there are also instances I've observed when, in trying to get tough, a parent loses the connection with a child altogether. One mom tearfully told me that in trying so hard to use the "tough love" principles, exactly like she thought she was being taught, she set her boundary in concrete. In getting tough, she cut off all contact with her son, even when she knew he was repentant and in recovery. She didn't add the love message. She lost the connection with her son and now several years later she wishes she had been taught more about the importance of balancing tough with tender.

Some don't understand that tough love principles are intended to stop the pain of problem behavior for both parties involved, like an emergency measure. It's a first step. Then it is necessary to look at deeper issues that need to be dealt with if we want to develop a healthy balance between tenderness and toughness over the long haul.

Should we set limits in concrete? Rarely. Healthy boundaries allow for flexibility and the healing process of both parties involved. Remember that in trying to get tough we can lose the connection altogether. We get too tough, and lose the love.

Then we become frustrated and feel as though we've failed. This approach works well when understood. But at times it still seems to fall short of helping us find a balance between tender and tough and fails to look at the deeper identity issues at work in us. It takes something more if we are to understand better who we were made to be as bearers of the image of God reflecting his balance between tender and tough.

The Integrated Tough Love Model
I have seen the need for an approach that provides more direction in showing how tenderness interplays with toughness in the parent-child relationship. Of course the urgency of a situation may necessitate our use of tough behavior before we have had sufficient time to develop a tough attitude that reflects tenderness, too. That is, we might need to act tough and be coached through the process until we are able to realize and own our ability to be tough. But understanding that getting back to the love message that is characterized by tenderness is critical. If a child at any age knows beyond a shadow of a doubt that he is loved, he can handle toughness. He has that reservoir of love built up inside of him from earlier tender treatment that he can draw upon. It allows him to hear the tough message and not feel abandoned or destroyed.

A child who does not have a reservoir of love down deep in him from which he can draw may take tough treatment as more rejection and even abandonment. A lack of consideration for the history of care that a child, or a mom, has received and internalized may wreak havoc in that relationship when tough lines are drawn.

45

Again, in tough love, the tough must always be balanced in the other person's perception with love—the other person must hear both, if it is to be effective.

One of the most important principles often overlooked is this: If the receiving person is only hearing tough, you must "amp up" the love.

If they are only hearing the love, and taking advantage of it, you "amp up" the tough.

If the other person does not receive both messages, it is either toughness *or* tenderness but it is not tough love. I have found that this is sometimes one of the missing pieces in understanding and successfully using tough love principles.

So for moms, learning how to act out the tough in tough love is only the beginning. We must take it a step further and integrate this external toughness with our internal tenderness, so that it begins to flow naturally out of a heart that has room for both.

God repeatedly shows in Scripture his love for us, love that is balanced, starting with his tender love that prepares us for his toughness. (We will look at specific passages in a later chapter.) He shows us the model, not to make us feel guilty as moms, but to show us how completely he loves us. It is his model of what it was that he wanted every human to experience when they came into this world. Like the little bird that mistakenly flew into my house and needed the toughness of capture that was best for him, God in his infinite compassion for us loves us tenderly and toughly—because it is best for us.

The other day as I watched my friend's daughter, Karen, deal with her son's issues about a party he wanted to attend, I was amazed to see that this mom just about had the tender-tough integration down pat. Karen's eleven-year-old son had been invited to a birthday party where they were going to also watch a movie. This mom had asked her son to find out which video was going to be shown. She discovered that the movie that the other parents had selected was questionable and did not meet her approval.

I listened as I heard Karen say to her son, "You know the rules. I have to see the movie first and then, if I approve, you can see it. But in this case, there is not enough time for me to do that and so I am going to have to say no to your watching it." Among her young son's pleas for a change in the rules, Karen made a compromise. "I will be glad to take you over to the party after the movie is finished. I know that it feels embarrassing to you to have to go into the party late, but you know how much I love you and therefore I am very careful about what you feed into your mind."

Karen's son made a face, objected with a few more sentences, and then went back to what he was doing, just as if nothing had happened. I know the history of what Karen's son has received in the way of tender treatment from his mom and I could almost see her son digging deep and tapping into his reservoir of love. It appeared that he came up with reassurance that "Mom surely must know best—she loves me so much." Karen's son heard both messages. He can accept her firmness because Karen had built into her son a place of love that gave her the authority to enforce her rules.

Most tenderhearted moms have built into their child that reservoir of love—that's what we are best at. But if you are not sure, find a place to start. It's hard for a child to take in the tough message if he does not have a history of tender treatment. Whether your child is a teenager or young adult it is never too late to start building into your child love that will help him respect your toughness.

There are some barriers when tenderhearted moms try to get tough. In our humanness, even knowing the needs our children have and wanting to move closer to God's model, most of us still struggle with how to stay tender and get tough enough. One of the reasons it's difficult is that there is such a wide range in our perceptions of what is tough enough and what is too tough. What one mom may consider as tough enough another may see as harsh and even cruel. Sometimes we don't recognize how much our personality bent affects how we see tender and tough. Thankfully, God in his wisdom did not make us all alike. Let's look now at how our personality shapes our efforts at integrating tenderness and toughness.

Thoughts to Consider:
A child needs to have both tender treatment and appropriate limits in order to feel loved and safe. The model that God sets forth, toughness set in the context of tenderness, provides the structure within which children of all ages can confidently and safely explore the world and learn independence.

What aspects mentioned here about tough love were new to you?

Which attempts to add toughness in the mothering role have been most familiar to you? Militaristic? Recovery? Integrated? Where did you hear these messages?

A Mom's Prayer

Dear Heavenly Father,

Sometimes it feels so confusing when I come up against the reality of the day-to-day interactions with my kids. I want to have the right balance between giving them the love they need and setting the limits I know are good for them, but often I am too permissive and then I lose my tender spirit and react out of anger and frustration. Then the tenderness is spoiled and the tough ends up being wrong, too. My kids don't get what they need and I worry that I am a failure at mothering. Please help me to learn to trust you for the right balance. Help me to understand more about how your tenderness and toughness are intertwined in how you deal with me.

In the name of Jesus,
Amen

Part Two

*Why It's Difficult for a
Tenderhearted Mom to Get Tough*

Chapter Three

Our Personality Bent May Lean Toward Being Tender

Telling a mom to raise her child by the book is a good idea, but you would have to have a different book for each mother and each child.

JULIE MAGUIRE

A baby cries in the grocery store. My ears perk up, and I am immediately drawn in. My first thought is, *Is someone there taking care of that little one? Does that child need help?*

An older lady is being treated rudely by a sales clerk. *Do I need to intervene? Can she work it out by herself or should I help?*

On the news I see pictured a dog that has been brutally beaten. My heart goes out to that vulnerable little animal.

I am a subjective, feeling-type person, and as a result, my feeling-oriented personality combined with my tender heart causes me at times to lean toward being too tender.

Whenever there is a need, it tugs at my heart. I wonder at times if it would be better if I could shut out all the things that are heart wrenching in order to protect my tender heart, and if that would be more comfortable? Would it be better if I were more objective?

My friend, Betty, who has also been my prayer partner for eighteen years, tells me that she seldom is drawn into situations like I am. She just simply doesn't pay attention to something that doesn't concern her. She is much more objective than I am. When she hears a baby cry, she thinks that, of course, someone else is probably there and she does not have to run and help. To help out an older person being treated rudely when she is not asked to, might be intrusive.

But if Betty is called on to help, she is just as willing as I am, and sometimes even more so. She has a wonderful caring gift of hospitality and I know that she has a tender heart—I have seen evidence of it many, many times. But her analytic thinking personality gives her an objectivity that I admire. She can be tougher in situations than I can. Objectivity that comes so naturally to Betty is much more difficult for me.

Another mom, who is more objective like my friend Betty, told me that she is tender at the core, but it is not easy for her to show her feelings. She said that when she sees another person doing all that soft "gushy" stuff, it seems a bit fake. It just doesn't come naturally to her and she finds that she is irritated with other moms who are too soft with their kids. She says that at times she might come across as too tough, but she thinks that her kids need that from her.

In contrast, moms who have a more subjective, feeling-style personality like me, are immediately drawn into situations because they feel so much for all those around them. We usually let you know right away that we care for you and will greet you with a warm open attitude. You will soon know that we have a need to keep everyone in our world happy and peaceful.

One subjective, feeling-style mom told me that no matter where she is she looks to see how others are doing and looks for how she might care for them. She says, "I know it might sound like I am codependent or something, but I have worked through that. I truly care and feel for the people around me."

We are those who have a tendency to be too tender at times.

Recently I happened to be in the kitchen of a friend, who has a more objective, thinking-style personality, when her seven-teen-year-old daughter was asking about buying her first car. Her daughter, Katy, who, in contrast to her mom, has a feeling style personality, was describing the perfect car that she had found. It was a little Volkswagen in a robin's egg blue color. She had fallen in love with it. This tough, objective mom was asking her more feeling, tender daughter if she had checked out several things. Had she checked the mileage on the car? Had she taken it to a garage to get an independent opinion about the condi-tion of the engine? Had she checked several other cars of the same model and year to see what the prices were? Had she figured out how she was going to make the payments?

By the time Katy's mom was finished with all the logical requirements needed to make a good purchase, Katy was in tears.

"But you don't understand, Mom, the only one I want is the blue one," she tearfully said.

In this case, mom and daughter were coming from entirely different perspectives as they dealt with the car question—Mom from a more objective viewpoint and Katy from a subjective per-spective. This is not to say that Katy did not need to listen and heed what her mom had to say, but Katy's perspective coming from her feelings needed to be valued as well. This mother-daughter interaction certainly pointed out the difference in personality between Katy and her mom.

What was tough enough and what was tender enough in this situation? Feeling-oriented Katy would draw the line in a very different place than her thinking mom.

Misunderstandings are difficult if we do not recognize that moms are not only different from each other, but often we moms are much different in personality than our children.

The Wide Range of Expression of Tenderness and Toughness

What makes us so different from each other, and how do we know how we come across to our children? Since every kid hears his mom differently, how do we know how much tenderness a particular child needs or how tough we need to be with a child so that from his perspective he is hearing us accurately?

One important factor in looking at how a mom can balance tenderness and toughness is to understand that there is a wide subjective range in the definition of what is tender and what is tough. We each have a different range to deal with in ourselves, and each of us has an individual perception of how we view it in others. What may seem appropriately tender to me may seem way too tender to another mom. It's the same with toughness. I may be alarmed by behavior that I see in a mom that I label as way too tough, while another mom sees it as not tough enough. However, most of us recognize the extremes.

I see moms who are so tender that they fail to set any limits for their children. They have become so permissive of any behavior or attitude that their children have nothing solid to bump up against or to kick off from. Their children cannot feel secure because there are no boundaries and therefore they cannot safely experience their own separateness. Other moms go to the opposite extreme. They lack tenderness to such a degree that their children experience them as harsh and cold. They can be tough, but their toughness is not tempered with tenderness. The consequences of being too tough can be equally as severe as being too tender. Moms who are too tough can leave their children feeling confused, insecure, and unable to find a place of warmth and comfort. Some moms do fit these extremes and we will look closer at the consequences of the extremes in the next section. But most of us find we are somewhere closer to the middle but still tend to err on one side or the other.

Understanding Our Differences

How did I become the kind of mother that I am? Many factors have great effect on how we mother and the personality we bring with us is one of them. It's extremely helpful to know what our "natural bent" is. Otherwise we often try to make correctional maneuvers but find that we soon fall right back into the same old routines that we are trying to break out of.

We get into trouble by expecting ourselves to follow a plan set out by others who show tenderness or toughness in certain ways without understanding that they may have started out in a very different place, and maybe with a different temperament than we did.

Depending on your personality, tenderness and toughness will be expressed in different ways. Are you the more objective, thinking mom who emphasizes more the teaching aspect of mothering and find that at times you tend to be too tough? Or are you a more subjective, feeling mom who emphasizes more the nurturing aspect of mothering and find that at times you tend to be too tenderhearted? Take this short tender-tough quiz to find out which style you lean toward.[1]

Tender-Tough Style Questionnaire

1. A trait that I value in myself most is:

_____A I am able to stay objective in emotionally laden situations.

_____B I am able to empathize with other people and see things from their viewpoint.

2. If I had a choice I would spend most of the time I have with my child helping him or her learn:

_____A How to size up situations and be able to analyze problems.

_____B How to read the responses of others and learn what their needs might be.

3. I have a difficult time with:

_____A Understanding other people's emotional responses.

_____B Staying objective in emotional situations.

4. The greatest compliment my child could give me is:

_____A That I taught him or her how to make decisions objectively.

_____B That I taught him or her that it is important to stay true to what they feel inside.

5. When faced with a decision, it is most important for me to:

_____A Think the situation through thoroughly, weighing the pros and cons.

_____B Consider the values at stake and which people might be helped or hurt.

6. My family would say that I am:

_____A More firm than gentle.

_____B More gentle than firm.

7. Which do you think is more important?

_____A To be just.

_____B To show mercy.

8. When do you feel the most satisfied?

_____A When you can discuss an issue thoroughly.

_____B When you can arrive at agreement on an issue.

9. Which is more important to you?

_____A Being consistent in what you say.

_____B Maintaining harmony with those around you.

Now add up the total number of A answers, and the total for the B answers. Record your answers in the spaces below:

My total number of A Answers: _____

My total number of B Answers: _____

If you have more A answers, you are probably more "thinking-oriented," and your giftedness lies in your objective analytical way of making decisions and resolving problems. Depending on how strong your score was, you will probably struggle more with being too tough than in being too tender as a mom.

If you have more B answers, you are probably more "feeling-oriented," and your giftedness lies more in the area of abilities to show sympathy and tenderness and decide things based on your feelings. You probably struggle more with being too tender.

While this score relates primarily to how we make decisions in our life—whether we are more objective or subjective decision makers—it is also highly correlated with tough-mindedness and tenderheartedness. Certainly every mom has some degree of toughness and some degree of tenderness, but she usually leans more toward one side or the other. Place an X on the continuum below at the place that represents your score.

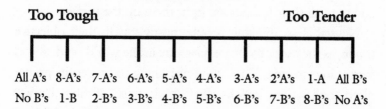

Too Tough   Too Tender

| All A's | 8-A's | 7-A's | 6-A's | 5-A's | 4-A's | 3-A's | 2'A's | 1-A | All B's |
| No B's | 1-B | 2-B's | 3-B's | 4-B's | 5-B's | 6-B's | 7-B's | 8-B's | No A's |

Scoring near the middle does not mean you don't struggle with how tender or how tough to be, but it could mean that finding a balance would come a little easier for you than for someone who scored nearer the ends of the continuum.

The Thinking Person

If you scored higher on the thinking side (more A's), you may appear to others to be cool and detached. This doesn't mean you don't have feelings, or that you don't care intensively for those you love—thinking people can be very tender at their core and do have deep feelings. But because of their objectivity, they do not show their deep feelings easily, or may choose to show their feelings to very few people.

One thinking-type mom told me that she operates with the assumption that her feelings reside in her brain—that she is very conscious about what feelings she lets show and that she regulates them very carefully. She says that her tenderness only came out occasionally and when it did, she was surprised by the intensity of it, and did not know how to handle it.

She is like other thinking moms who tell me that they can be objective about almost anything except their own kids. They say that they cover their feelings with their objectivity until something really critical comes along concerning one of their children and then all their feelings are right there on the surface.

Nevertheless, thinking people mostly stay in their objective mode, as they seek to create harmony in the world of ideas and factual information. They want everything to fit into its proper place, so they often look for the formula, or set of rules, that will make everything fit together, even as they mother their children.

Thinking people base their decisions on objective data. They are always searching for truth, and tend to have a more black-and-white viewpoint on life. If something seems to be in the gray area, the thinking person simply believes that they just haven't gathered enough data. They think that if they can just look further, they will discover the truth.

Approximately one-third of all women and two-thirds of all men score on the thinking side of this scale, which forms the basis for men being stereotyped as more analytical. Those who score on this side of the scale tend to be more tough-minded in their approach to situations and relationships. Therefore, women who score on this side of the scale tend to struggle more with showing their tenderhearted side, especially in the eyes of those they are close to.

Thinking-style moms have to become especially aware of how powerful they may come across to their kids. Thinking people make decisions based on objective criteria, just as Katy's mom was trying to get her daughter to do. They usually have three or four points for everything and pride themselves in having their thoughts very organized. They often intimidate feeling-oriented people with their ability to analyze and sometimes overpower others with their logic.

The Feeling Person

If you came out on the feeling side of the graph (more B's), you make decisions in a personal way, based more on a subjective value system rather than objective criteria. Most of life, for the feeling person, is concerned with how their decisions and behaviors will affect other people. A decision is good if everyone's feelings have been taken into consideration. They work hard at being liked and appreciated by others and as a result, will obviously struggle with being more tender-hearted than tough-minded.

Approximately two-thirds of all women and one-third of all men score on the feeling side of this scale, giving rise to the social stereotype of women being more emotional than men. It also leads to part of the reason why more women than men struggle with being too tenderhearted.

A feeling-oriented mom once told me that she felt that no one understood all the feeling that she had to give to others. She said that she always wants to help her adult kids because she cares so much for them and that at times no one needs or wants her help. She said that she felt as though her very best trait, her tender heart, did not seem to be appreciated by her family.

If you are primarily a feeling mom, you will always be seeking harmony among the people who are important to you. The happiness of the other persons you care about is a strong value, so you will often expend massive amounts of energy to see that people are properly "in place" in relation to one another. If a feeling mom has a thinking child, she will probably find that he gets impatient with her, as her thinking child wants to just get on with something rather than talk about how he feels about it.

As a feeling mom the tendency is to see all sides of another's problem to the point of making excuses for another's behavior even when it is not appropriate. Feeling people are always trying to explain the behavior of others. They want to be fair about things, but their sense of fairness is related to emotions, not to actions. So sometimes they come across as "defending the enemy," so to speak, in their effort to try to get others to see all sides of an issue.

Your score on this scale has a lot to do with how you struggle with the tender-tough dilemma. But since being tenderhearted or tough-minded is really a relative term, it also depends to some degree on how you are perceived by your own children and other family members. Let's look at how this plays out in children.

Who Is My Child?

The Thinking Child

The thinking child, like the objective mom, will make his decisions mainly through his intellect. He will make detached, logical, and objective decisions. He will analyze the information he has gathered and then decide what to do based on rationality.

A favorite question of the thinking child is "Why?" If Mom tries to short-circuit the "why," the child may stop asking the question out loud, but still wonder inside as he has a great need for an answer. Thinking children may have an affinity for classes such as science and math. They love to debate and can often take up the challenge on either side of the argument. They will work very hard at being correct, and this need can sometimes get them in trouble, since they may appear to sacrifice a relationship for the sake of rightness.

The emotional side of the thinking child certainly exists even though he doesn't talk about it. Jim, a thinking child, was accompanying his feeling friend, Bill, on an outing to Disneyland. In the car on the way there, Bill was so excited he could hardly contain himself. He was bouncing in his seat, excitedly talking about the rides and what they would do that day. Jim sat there so quietly that Bill's dad asked if he was excited about the day. Jim said, "I sure am. I'm just as excited as Bill." He just didn't show it on the outside.

The quieter thinking child likes to work on individual projects, as this gives him the opportunity to evaluate his own performance more accurately. When playing games with friends, or with the family, the rules of the game are very important to the thinking child. Even before he really understands what the rules are, he may be talking about the "rules" of the game.

For the thinking child, mom can never be too tough, as long as she is fair. Fairness is always an issue. Mom may think that she is being fair, but the thinking child is quick to let her know what his idea of "fair" is. A more feeling, tenderhearted mom may come across to her thinking child as "wishy-washy" instead of tender because the thinking child is looking for more objectivity. Or when Mom thinks she is being tough with the thinking child, he may still be experiencing her as too tenderhearted. Sometimes the mom can be so tenderhearted with the thinking child that he believes Mom doesn't really care or understand the issues. So the feeling mom with a thinking child would do well to take the time to try to understand her child's viewpoint on how he is treated. Remember, a thinking child needs to respect his mom and he will quickly find that respect if she is able to in turn respect his need for fairness and answers.

The Feeling Child

The feeling child, like the feeling adult, makes his best decisions based on personal values and the impact that a decision will have on friends and family members. Rather than worry about the "why" of a situation, the feeling child wonders about who might be upset in the situation. As a result, the feeling child will often find it difficult to say what he means. His tenderheartedness will cause him to automatically soften what he is saying.

The feeling child is more outwardly sensitive than the thinking child. He is more dependent on external affirmations. When a teacher or a parent doesn't praise good work, the feeling child will take it personally, even to the point of thinking he is not liked. As a result, criticism and harsh punishment can be devastating to the feeling child. Often the only discipline needed is a raised eyebrow or a harsh look.

From an early age, the feeling child is gifted in his ability to understand other people. He can feel the discomfort of the new kid in the classroom, and can just as easily feel the tension in the home if Mom and Dad are having troubles. As a result, he will work very hard at creating harmony on the playground and in the home.

Competition is not important to the feeling child. He is more concerned about the relationships in a game than in the score. The same goes for rules, which are so important to the thinking child. To the feeling child, rules can spoil the fun of the game and the camaraderie that is being sought in playing the game.

Rather than work alone on a project, the feeling child would much rather work on group projects. He may feel especially good that everyone in the group gets the same grade as their working together may have helped raise the grade of someone in the group.

For the feeling child, a thinking mom may come across as too tough in the same situation where the thinking child believes Mom is just being fair. The objectivity of the thinking mom will be lost in the subjective experience of the feeling child. It doesn't take much for the feeling child to interpret Mom's behavior as being too tough and harsh. So the mom of the feeling child would do well to take the time to try to understand how her child may be interpreting the treatment he is receiving from her.

A Checklist for Your Child[2]

You might want to photocopy these lists so you can complete one for each child. Put an "X" by the trait that you see more often in each child.

THE THINKING CHILD WILL MORE OFTEN	**THE FEELING CHILD WILL MORE OFTEN**
__ be concerned with fairness	__ be concerned with others' feelings
__ ask "why" questions and press for answers	__ try to understand and explain others' actions
__ be objective	__ be subjective
__ love to debate with you	__ not want to hurt you, so usually won't debate
__ see competition as desirable and necessary	__ see competition as secondary to relationships
__ fight to be right	__ be good at peacemaking
__ enjoy analyzing things	__ show feelings in facial expressions
__ treat rules as primary in games and what others feel about them as secondary	__ treat people's feelings as primary in games and rules as secondary

As you consider the personality of each of your children, note how they operate in relation to your own preference for either feeling or thinking. Talk with your husband about your evaluation and see if he agrees. Then keep in mind the differences and how that affects the way each child experiences you as more tenderhearted or more tough-minded.

Knowing how we got where we are can help us present ourselves honestly and accurately before God as he provides a way for us to find his balance in us. Our personality plays an important role in this process. We want to look now at how what we brought with us from our own childhoods affects what kind of mothers we become. We will see how important our mothering heritage is as it provides a basis for how we view both tenderness and toughness.

Thoughts to Consider:
Learning whether our personality bent leans more toward the objective thinking trait or more toward the subjective feeling trait can give us insight into how we may come across to our kids as more tough or more tender. Looking at our children's personality traits can help us understand why one child may need more tender care from us, while another child may need us to be more tough.

How do you think understanding whether you are more feeling-oriented or more thinking-oriented will help you better understand some of the difficulties you have in balancing tenderness and toughness in dealing with your children?

Describe one thing you might do differently with each child as a result of knowing whether they are more feeling- or thinking-oriented?

A Mom's Prayer

Dear Heavenly Father,

Thank you for making me the way I am as part of your majestic creation. I want to appreciate the personality you placed in me, and so will you help me to use the giftedness in it to honor you? Many times I fail to take the time to recognize and appreciate my children's personality traits. Help me to see them for the unique creations that you meant them to be. Help me to accept the ways they are different from me and give me the patience to nurture those differences in them. I want them to be prepared to love you with all their hearts and to live the life you have in mind for them.

In Jesus' name,
Amen

Chapter Four

The Influence of Our Mothering Heritage

Listen to me, all who hope for deliverance—all who seek the Lord! Consider the quarry from which you were mined, the rock from which you were cut! Yes, think about your ancestors.

ISAIAH 51:1-2a

Sometimes the influence of my mom shows up in the little things, like when I find myself doing some insignificant thing exactly like she did. Just recently I was out shopping and looking at a skirt that I was considering buying. I looked around a bit more and then returned to the original garment and thought it looked quite pretty and decided the style was right. Then without even thinking I took a small handful of the fabric the skirt was made of and crushed it in my hand and then quickly released it. I wanted to see how resilient the fabric was to wrinkling. It suddenly struck me that I had seen my mom do that many, many times. My mom was a wonderful seamstress and often I went with her to shop for a piece of fabric to make a new dress for me or my sisters. As we would walk down the aisles lined with bolts of fabrics she would consider one, and then came the ultimate test. She would take a little of the fabric in her hand, squeeze it, and then release it to see if it wrinkled too easily. Resistance to wrinkling was much more important than the pattern or color. If it didn't pass the test she would turn to me and say, "This is not the one. We have to look further."

Sometimes I don't realize that I am doing something like my mom. It really surprises me when it is pointed out, but it certainly doesn't surprise my family. Like the other day when I offered someone a portion of food for the third or maybe it was the fourth time. I just wanted to make sure that they meant it when they said "no" the first time. My kids just looked at each other with that knowing look that says, "There she goes again. She's acting just like Grandma."

And sometimes the influence of my mom shows up in the big things, like in how I deal with the stresses of life, or how I act as a wife or a mother. The other day when I reacted to something one of my kids said, I immediately heard my mom's voice from years past saying the very same thing. Undoubtedly our mom's influence on us is great whether it be positive or negative.

"Don't ask me about my relationship with my mom," Jamie, a mom in her forties said. "I will cry and I don't want to cry— I've already dealt with it and I don't know why it still affects me." Women have a hunch that what they experienced with their own moms in the past is affecting their present, but most are unaware of the deep impact it has on how they live day by day.

One anxious mom said, "I am terrified that I will become like her! I hate it when I catch myself saying or doing something exactly like my mom did. She and my dad divorced when I was three and from that time on I knew that I was a bother to her. She was really abusive to me and my brother—both physically and emotionally. Either I got the brunt of her frustration or my brother did, but I think she was harder on me. At times she whipped me so severely that I could not go to school. And then that made her even madder. I am so afraid that I will hit my daughter when I get angry. I pray every day that I will never treat my child like I was treated."

Often I have the privilege to speak to the many Mothers of Preschoolers (MOPS) groups and other young mom's groups around southern California. These moms usually don't have a lot of time for reflection about what they received or did not receive from their own moms because they are mostly operating in, as one mom put it, "pure survival mode." Most of them are trying to just make it through their hectic day. But this particular morning I was going to talk about the different mothering styles and what the relationship with our own mother might have to do with the kind of mother we become. For their discussion time I asked the two hundred or so moms who were sitting around tables to think on this question: "Do you think that moms tend to repeat the mothering style that they received from their own mother, or are they more likely to go to the opposite extreme and mother their own children very differently?"

At one table I sat in on the discussion. Animated conversation started right away.

Barb was quick to jump in. "Well, I'll start. I had a good mom. Sometimes I hesitate to say that because I know that some of you had a really rough relationship with your moms. But I remember that my mom was really good with my sister and me. I don't mean that we never fought or that she never got mad at us, but we always knew that Mom was there for us and that she loved us very much. Yes, I think I would repeat a lot of what my mom did with me in the way of mothering. Now as a mom myself, I appreciate her even more. My mom and I have become great friends and give each other lots of support."

Two or three other moms nodded in agreement, and offered positive things that they felt they would repeat from a mother they felt had done a pretty good job in raising them.

Then Julie hesitantly asked, "But what if your mom did *not* give you a positive model for mothering? My mom definitely was not a good mother. As a child I never knew what kind of mood she was going to be in from one day to the next. It was like she had this love-hate relationship with me. To this day nothing I do seems to be good enough, and she is very verbal in her criticism of me. I have felt put down by her my whole life. I don't want to do that with my kids. Am I doomed to follow in her footsteps?"

Another mom agreed with Julie. "My mom was angry with me, it felt like, most of my life. She was on my case nearly every day for something. I felt very controlled by her and even now I have a hard time being around her. I certainly hope I don't repeat that with my own kids."

Cheryl brought another viewpoint. "My mom was not around much so I was left with babysitters a lot and then in like the third grade I was left alone most of the time. My mom had to work and I know how important her job was to her. I think she did the best she could with me. As a single mom, she had to have the income. I didn't have anyone to depend on, so I learned very early how to take care of myself and I know that I am probably more independent than most as a result. However, I think that now I have been educated enough to know that my baby needs more than my mom gave to me and I try hard to do it differently. But when I find myself shutting off my emotions when things get tough, I get afraid that I am repeating her attitude in some subtle way."

Why Look Back

When these moms took the time to think about it, they found that they definitely had opinions about how their moms had mothered them. Most of us do have some memory of how we were treated as a child, and at times wonder what it has to do with the way we live out our lives in the present. Even if we remember very little or have never taken the time to allow ourselves to look at our childhood for fear we might uncover things that we do not want to know, we are somewhat curious about how it has affected us. One mom said, "I don't want to know how my childhood has affected me! I don't go for all this looking at the past stuff. If I dwell on it I might repeat some of the negative things unconsciously. I don't need that right now." Later this same mom admitted that she would like to know more about how she had been influenced by her mom, but she was afraid that she might tarnish the images she has of her mom *and* dad as the good parents she was sure they must have been.

At times I have thought the same thing. Why would I want to look at the negative things in my childhood, and maybe dwell on them instead of on the positives? In doing so, would I be blaming my mom or casting a bad light on her that was not necessary? I didn't want to do that. My mom was a sweet, loving, gentle woman who came from a terribly abusive family. In spite of her own painful heritage she somehow managed to give me and my brothers and sisters a large part of what we needed. But there were things that she was not able to give. Some of those things have left gaps that seem to be at the root of the trouble I have had in learning how to integrate toughness into my tenderness when it is needed. But shouldn't I appreciate what I did receive and forget the rest—leaving well enough alone?

It is wonderful to appreciate what we did receive. And yet we are called on to examine ourselves in order to grow and become more Christlike. That may mean that we have to explore why there are problem patterns of thinking, feeling, or behavior that keep popping up in our lives even when we have tried our hardest to eliminate them. So we go back and forth from trying hard to change things, and feeling discouraged when we don't see any results, to keeping ourselves so busy that we don't have to think about the problem until it shows up again.

Many of the things we are trying to change have their roots in our past experiences, many times in needs that were not met when we were children. What was missing is important—important to understand if we are to bring it to the Lord and allow God's healing presence to enter into that area. He wants us to allow his power to make changes that will not just be temporary, but changes that will affect us for life.

No mother is able to give everything a child needs and so there will be gaps, no matter what. So all of us have things in our pasts that affect us. Someone once said to me, "Can't I just ask God to cover it all and where there are things that I needed, just ask him to fill in there? Do I really have to know or understand what was missing?" That certainly would be easier than looking at it, and sometimes he does choose to do it that way. But I have found that more often than not, God expects us to understand the things that we bring to him, to know what it is that we are asking healing for.

The Enduring Effects of Mom

As we look at our own beginnings, about what we have received or not received in the way of care that would have been the best for us, we may be surprised at how many areas of our lives have been affected by Mom. Jeanne Hendricks, a mother of four, describes the impact she had on her own children's lives. She writes:

> My children tell me that at those times when I was no more than a photograph on the dresser two thousand miles away, I talked in their consciences. I showed up in their habits and decisions. I was there in a front row seat. What an assignment!
>
> In everything from the high chair routine to the bridal parties, I had been teaching something ... and I had the inside track. Because I was "Mom," I was different; I walked in their hearts whether I wanted to or not. It was critically important that I went in the right direction, that I used my own devotion to package God's love for them.[1]

Jeanne is describing the process of how we internalize what we experience from Mom, that is, how we take into ourselves the voice, attitude, and behaviors of our mother. We see who we are from what we take in from her. Later we internalize behaviors and attitudes of other significant adults in our lives. But no one is as influential as mother, because she is there first. When her treatment is characterized by tender responses, we learn that we can trust and feel safe. When tenderness is missing, or is inconsistent, we feel anxious and insecure. Drs. Henry Cloud and John Townsend point out in *The Mom Factor* that "not only do we learn our patterns of intimacy, relating, and separateness from mother, but we also learn about how to handle failure, troublesome emotions, expectations and ideals, grief and loss, and many of the other components that make up our 'emotional IQ'—that part of us that guarantees whether or not we will be successful at love and work."[2]

What we received from Mom, or our other primary caregiver, will have a definite effect on us one way or another. What a blessing it is when we are able to reap the benefits of a mother who was able, not to be perfect, but to be "good enough." But when there are deficits in how we were mothered, our picture of ourselves gets distorted. Then we struggle with defining what we think or feel and consequently struggle with boundary issues that affect how we mother our own children. Negative patterns in relationships get promoted that we may repeat in relationships all our lives, patterns that keep us from seeing what is tender enough and what is tough enough not only in our mothering but in all of our relationships.

So it is reasonable that we are curious about our first relationship because we already suspect that the interaction between our parents and us, especially with our mothers, has a lot to do with how things go in our adult lives. Those who study babies in their first years have managed to give us a lot of information to help us understand that earliest relationship with Mom and its later effects. We now know that a child who is abused is very likely to become a child abuser. We know that a child who had a very tenuous insecure attachment to his mom will have great difficulty feeling secure in his adult relationships. Robert Karen in his book, *Becoming Attached*, said, "Some of us repeat futile patterns with intimates, mates, and children to the point where we may question whether we are capable of close, satisfying relationships at all. At times it feels as if the shadow of our parents hangs over us like a fate we cannot elude. And we wonder: How much do our childhoods, and especially the quality of our first loving bonds, determine whether we can get love right as adults?"[3]

Keeping the Focus

In looking at missing or negative aspects in how you were mothered, if you are like me, you will immediately evaluate how you are mothering your own kids and judge yourself negatively. Again, keep in mind that we cannot possibly meet all our children's needs nor can we be perfect mothers. So resist the temptation to judge yourself and keep the focus for the time being on what you received as a child. In a later chapter we will look at how you might change some things in your relationship with your own kids. But here, think of it this way: It is as if you as the infant, came into this world holding a cup in your tiny hands. You wanted and needed for someone to fill your cup with the things that would make you feel safe and loved. You wanted positive responses and acceptance. You wanted Mom to be available and wanted her to participate in your life. You needed her tender treatment and her loving toughness, too. Your needs were great, probably greater than your mom's ability to meet them. Consequently, you may have gotten less in your cup than you needed, leaving some places that still need to be filled in.

This is our focus for the next four chapters—looking at how a child attaches and at three of the basic needs that we had as children. These needs, when met, formed the foundation upon which we could build a healthy concept of the world and ourselves. We needed to feel *safe enough* that we could trust, *loved enough* to feel valued, and *accepted enough* to feel confident. When there is enough of these, our cup is filled and we will feel secure enough to deal satisfactorily with the world. When there is not enough, all areas of our lives are affected. The problem area that we are looking at specifically is this: How we struggle with appropriate integration of toughness into our tenderness and how our confidence in setting appropriate boundaries for our children and ourselves gets undermined when we have places in our cups that are unfilled.

Perspective Is Important

It's important to keep in perspective why we look at the past. We look back to get an understanding of what we brought into adulthood with us, always with the goal to bring God's perspective to it. We seek healing where healing is needed, and allow God to empower us to forgive those who were inadequate or hurtful. There is a verse in the Old Testament book of Job that says,

> Please inquire of past generations,
> And consider the things searched out by their fathers.
> For we are only of yesterday and know nothing,
> Because our days on earth are as a shadow.
>
> JOB 8:8-10, NASB

In this dialogue between Bildad and Job, Bildad is referring to a concept that is thousands of years old—that our past can teach us about our present if we let it. Our pasts can bring understanding that will help us change our present. We may wish that we could have had a closer relationship with Mom or maybe we wish that we could have had less of Mom. Either way, understanding it helps us see how our cup may not have been filled with the right quality or right amount of tender treatment.

Dr. Dennis Guernsey and Lucy Guernsey in their book, *Birthmarks,*[4] remind us of several principles to guide us in looking at the past. First, we must recognize that the power of the past, though it may be awesome, does not need to be fearsome for a child of God. Second, they remind us to look for explanations rather than excuses. Third, we are to recognize that while the past influences our present, it does not determine it. And fourth, they remind us to look for both positive and negative examples in our pasts. Remember that our past—and in particular here we are speaking of how we were mothered—influences greatly what we do in the present, but it does not mean that we are doomed to repeat it. We, by the grace of God, can change the patterns that might have been set in motion by our mothers and even before them, by our grandmothers.

If we keep an open heart, we may be surprised at how God wants to use our pasts to heal us in the present.

Thoughts to Consider:
Because our moms had such a great influence on us, it is important to let our past teach us by pointing out what might have been amiss in our care so that we can better understand what we brought with us into the present. Only then can we bring ourselves with our unmet needs to God and allow him to fill our cups and make us whole.

What do you think Isaiah meant when he said, "Consider the rock from which you were cut and the quarry from which you were hewn" (Is 51:1)?

What are some of the effects of that first relationship with your mom (or primary caregiver) that you can identify as still operating in your life today?

A Mom's Prayer

Dear Heavenly Father,

    Help me to make a realistic appraisal of the childhood you allowed me to have so that I might see where healing needs to take place. Some of what I received from my mom seems to be less than what would have been best for me. Will you help me to see the gaps where maybe tenderness or toughness was lacking or was excessive, and help me to see how to break away from patterns in my life that may have resulted from the treatment I received. I don't want those patterns to keep me from experiencing the best you have for me. I want every aspect of my life to reflect your goodness and your love, but sometimes I have a hard time recognizing the destructive things that I repeat from my past. Thank you for being lovingly available, responsive to my needs and always accepting of me when I need it most.

In the name of Jesus,
Amen

Part Three

What We Needed From Our Moms

Chapter Five

Our First Lesson in Tenderness

Piglet sidled up to Pooh from behind.
"Pooh!" he whispered.
"Yes, Piglet?"
"Nothing," said Piglet, taking Pooh's paw.
"I just wanted to be sure of you."

A.A. MILNE

"Mama?" I remember one of my young sons would call to me from another room. I would answer, "Yes? What do you need?" No reply. Just silence. I would answer again and once again there would be no reply. Then I would stop whatever I was doing and go to where he was playing and say, "I am right here. Are you OK?" Usually he would just look up and smile. I realized many years later that he simply wanted to be reassured that I was there, close by, satisfied by the tone of my response that he was important and that I was available if he needed me. Like Piglet, he wanted to be sure of me.

The importance of Mom's presence and her responses is delightfully illustrated in one of my favorite children's books, *Are You My Mother?*[1] Its author, P.D. Eastman, tells of a baby bird's search for his mother. While the mother bird is gone from the nest in search of food, her baby misses her. He tries to fly, but falls out of the nest. So he decides to search for his mother.

On his journey, he encounters among other things, a kitten, a hen, a dog, and a steam shovel. He asks each one in turn, "Are you my mother?" When he realizes that none of them is his mother, he exclaims in frustration, "I did have a mother. I know I did!" Then he cries, "I have to find her. I will. I WILL!" When the steam shovel lifts him back into the nest where he is reunited with his mom he exclaims with pride, "You are a bird, and you are my mother." What relief! Mom is again available and close by. And the look on mama bird's face seems to show her positive response, as she lovingly comforts her little nestling. He knew he was OK. He knew he belonged to someone. Baby bird was learning about his worth as he saw himself reflected in Mom's beaming countenance—he was valuable and worthy of her presence.

As children, every one of us wanted to know that Mom was there for us when we needed her, whether our need was physical or emotional. If she was there, the security of her presence took away our lonely feelings, and her tender response to our needs made us feel safe as we began to learn how to trust.

I can remember the anguish that I went through years ago, while working as a nursery school teacher, trying to console little students who were not at all ready to be separated from their moms. I will never forget one little girl named Liz. Liz had endeared herself to all of us who worked at the school. She was inconsolable for an hour or so after her mom left her there, day after day. When it came to naptime each day, Liz panicked, seeming to think that if she went to sleep it meant that she would miss Mom's coming. She never let anyone touch her shoes, letting us know that her shoes had to stay on in case

Mom came. We tried to make her as safe and secure as we could by holding her and comforting her, but little Liz was guarded and let us know that our presence was no substitute for Mom's.

Our First Relationship

The importance of the mother is obvious, especially while the fetus is developing in the womb. In fact, mother and fetus have a perfect symbiotic relationship during this time, being attached to each other through the umbilical cord. The womb provides the ideal nurturing environment. It's warm and quiet—all sounds are muffled. Mom's heart is softly beating to a rhythm that comforts and soothes. Needs are met even before they are experienced. For the most part, it is an idyllic place to be.

But then comes the trauma of birth, and what immediately follows birth. I recently watched as our new little granddaughter, Robyn, was born. I saw her as she was carried from the birthing room to the nursery, only minutes old. They took her to a brightly lit nursery—in spite of the fact that she had been living in total darkness for nine months. They first wiped her clean, then put some drops in her eyes, even gave her an injection, stretched her so they could measure her, then weighed her and took foot-prints. Of course, the nurses were very gentle and careful, but prior to this, nothing had ever touched her. Quite a welcome into the world!

Then they wrapped little Robyn tightly and placed her in a bassinet and she fell asleep. Then something else happened— she experienced a need, something she had never experienced before. She felt hunger. She cried for someone to come. She was already finding that living in this new world could be difficult, except for one thing, Mom was there. And so, at the same time Robyn set about to get her newly experienced needs met, she also started on another task. She was forming an attachment to the person she believed would make this strange world feel safe for her—to the mother who would be responsive to her. She already knew her voice. Her smell was familiar. And it felt wonderful to be cuddled and held close to Mom's body once again. The heartbeat was still there! She was safe. She was experiencing relationship and tenderness for the very first time. Like little Robyn, we as babies began an intricate "dance" as we communicated our needs and wanted and expected Mom to lovingly move in response to meet them.

The need we had to find safety with a person we could trust in this strange new world was critical. It was basic to our development. We thrived on it. If things went well between our mom and us, we found in our relationship to her a safe place that was warm and comforting, what psychologist John Bowlby[2] and his associates called a secure base. He likened a child's secure base to a military base. From his secure home base, the child can go on exploring expeditions to check out the unfamiliar, "the enemy," while confidently aware that the base is always there if he needs to retreat. Back at his secure base he can regroup, be nourished, and get ready to go out again. He dares to take risks, knowing that Mom (and hopefully, Dad) is waiting for him at his secure base. Canadian psychologist Mary Ainsworth, an associate of Bowlby, wrote, "The mother seems to provide a secure base from which these excursions can be made without anxiety."[3] The more confident a child is that his base is secure, that someone is there ready to catch him if he falls or fails, the more secure he feels in exploring the world. What is most interesting is that the mother's role as provider of food and physical needs is generally irrelevant to the concept of a secure base. What helps to make the base secure is the mother's ability to consistently provide a haven of comfort and protection.

Bowlby believed the infant actively seeks and needs not only the safety Mom provides but wants affectionate relationship and looks to Mom (or the father or another primary caregiver if Mom isn't there) for the fulfillment of that need. Bowlby wrote:

"When a baby is born he cannot tell one person from another and indeed can hardly tell person from thing. Yet, by his first birthday he is likely to have become a connoisseur of people. Not only does he come quickly to distinguish familiars from strangers but amongst his familiars he chooses one or more favorites. They are greeted with delight; they are followed when they depart; and they are sought when absent. Their loss causes anxiety and distress; their recovery, relief and a sense of security. On this foundation, it seems, the rest of his emotional life is built—without this foundation there is risk for his future happiness and health."[4]

Attachment to Mom

Every child forms some type of attachment with the mothering figure. For many of us, we attached and fell in love with Mom and hopefully Mom fell in love with us, too. If Mom tried hard not to let us down, we began to experience the world as friendly and positive. We saw ourselves as good and valuable. We were then able to build our first positive models of ourselves and others. It was the beginning of a secure attachment that would provide the foundation for a lifetime of healthy relationships.

In seeking to better understand the early attachment a child forms to his mother, interested researchers in the last four decades have directed much of their efforts toward study in that area. Early studies by ethnologist Konrad Lorenz in the 1930s on the process of imprinting among baby ducks served as the inspiration for further study in attachment. Lorenz believed that a baby duck's tendency to follow after its mom soon after hatching insured that he would form a strong bond with Mom, and keep her close by. He attached to her. Lorenz also found that because a duckling attaches itself to the first moving thing it sees, if he became that moving object, the duckling became hopelessly attached to him and would follow him everywhere he went. He had become its mom!

Psychologist John Bowlby observed similar attachment behaviors in human infants. He noted that although we as babies cannot waddle after our mothers like baby ducks, we are equipped with other attachment behaviors used to get Mom's attention. We cry and soon start to smile, babble, reach, and grasp. In fact, we are born with a whole set of built-in behaviors that help draw Mom in—behaviors that are designed to insure her active participation in the attachment process. If our mom was able to respond positively to our expressed need for relationship, the foundation was formed for the development of a wonderful emotional bond between mother and child.

The work of Bowlby and other researchers has helped explain how important this primary attachment is as it continues to influence and shape future relationships. They found that an infant will attach to Mom or whomever is most present in some way. The built-in behaviors meant to draw Mom in are meant to work to help Mom respond so that her child can establish a secure attachment to her. In 1961, Ainsworth and her colleagues explored the importance of the way in which a mother responds to her baby, and began to look at the quality of that response as having a strong effect on how that infant attaches to Mom. They saw that Mom's responses greatly influenced how her baby experienced the world and they were the basis for the first images that he formed of himself. Ainsworth conducted years of extensive studies of the interaction between infant and mother during the infant's first year of life and identified the development of different patterns in the ways an infant attached to mother. She found one secure pattern and two types of insecure patterns of attachment. These attachment patterns are formed particularly in the first twelve months and are largely based on the quality of the responses an infant gets from Mom. From these patterns of experience, the way the infants were responded to, each child formed what Ainsworth called "internal working models" of themselves and others. From that model they would later develop a perception about the world, a perception that persists into adulthood.

The Secure Attachment

Ainsworth described one type as a *secure attachment*. She found that infants who were securely attached had moms who were able to consistently respond to their infants with a warm, tender, sensitive, and dependable style. When their babies cried, they picked up the signal and responded lovingly. The result in their infants was that they became confident and felt the world was a safe place for them to be because Mom was available and she responded. These babies began to feel that their moms could be counted on and would be there for them in a warm, nurturing way to meet their physical and emotional needs.

Ainsworth also wanted to see how a child reacted when briefly separated from Mom and how a child reacted upon reunion with his mom. She found that when the securely attached child was separated from Mom, he cried and showed distress, showing how much he needed her, but when Mom returned, he warmly greeted her and reached to be held and cuddled by her. If Mom responded he was soothed by her warm comforting responses. Then after a short time he was ready to get down to play again.

In follow-up studies, the securely attached infant was found to carry with him through childhood and into adulthood the positive residue of Mom's early tender responses.

Insecure Attachments

But what if Mom was not able or was unwilling to respond in positive ways to the needs of her child? Ainsworth identified two patterns of attachment that she saw as insecure. The first she described as an *anxious-ambivalent* attachment. The mothers of these infants were very unpredictable. These moms responded with warm sensitivity and loving tenderness at times and at other times treated their infants with cool indifference.

Sometimes the moms were downright mean to their babies. Even if these moms were available to their infants, their unpredictable responses kept their infants guessing about whether their mom would be loving and positive or cold and uncaring. These infants seemed to be more anxious about where Mom was and about how she was going to respond to them.

From what I have learned since about how babies attach to their moms, I know from her anxious, watchful attitude that my little nursery school student, Liz, may have been attached to her mom in an anxious-ambivalent way. Liz's mom probably was unpredictable in her care for Liz. But in those days, none of us understood that. We just knew that we wanted to sit and hold her and try to make her as safe and secure as we could. We knew she wanted to be close to her mom, and we knew that Liz was very worried about her relationship with Mom.

The ambivalently attached child may have experienced his treatment as smothering or controlling, sticky and somewhat patronizing at times and harsh and cold at other times. The ambivalently attached child cannot relax in the tender care of his mother because he doesn't know what her responses might be in the next moment or two. Ainsworth found that moms—like Liz's mom may have been—were nice people, but in their interaction with their child, they had difficulty responding in a warm and consistent way. They were out-of-sync with what the baby needed. These moms could be sarcastic or irritated with normal childlike behavior much more often than mothers of securely attached babies. Sometimes these mothers were rough in their handling of the infant—much more frequently than the mothers of secure infants were—and later they often tried to control situations by threats to abandon the child. For example, one mom told her toddler, "You better be good, or I will leave you here." Another threatened to leave the house if her child did not behave. These moms seemed surprised when they were told that those kinds of threats caused extreme panic and pain in their child.

When separated from Mom, Ainsworth found that the ambivalently attached baby showed anxiety, anger, and clinginess while she was gone, but in spite of wanting Mom desperately when she returned, he arched away stiffly or went limp as Mom tried unsuccessfully to soothe him. He pushed away what he desperately wanted to have.

The ambivalently attached infant carried with him throughout childhood his anxious, worried style and observers found that even in adulthood, there were evidences of the effect of mom's earlier unpredictable responses.

The second insecure type Ainsworth identified was the *anxious-avoidant* attachment. These children experienced a lack of response with real emotional abandonment or outright rejection from Mom. They learned early that to put out normal attaching behaviors like crying and reaching to be held, brought a rejecting attitude from Mom. So they shut down those behaviors, learning that those behaviors only disturbed Mom and drove her away. So in order to maintain closeness in proximity to Mom, they learned to shut down their need—they found they could only stay close to Mom if they were not so needy.

Some mothers of avoidantly attached babies did not seem to enjoy a lot of physical touching of their child. There were few warm cuddly responses from these mothers, as they did not hold their child close to their body for long periods of time and often let their child stay for extended periods of time alone in their crib. These children learned early on to be very self-sufficient and appeared on the surface to be well adjusted and independent. But a closer look told the tale of a child who was warding off emotional pain by learning not to depend on anyone for anything.

Ainsworth found that when separated from Mom, the avoidantly attached child was distressed and upset, but when Mom returned he was somewhat put off by her and seemed to avoid her attempts to soothe him. He seemed unresponsive to being held and yet he cried when he was put down.

The avoidantly attached infant was observed to carry his painful self-sufficiency into childhood and in adulthood was found to have shut down most needs. This left him with an independent attitude that kept others at a distance.

Recently, I attended a meeting where a lot of women were present—some were older and some were young mothers with babies. I watched as a young mom struggled to quiet her little one who had been quite fussy throughout the evening. This young mom's mother was also present and was seated next to her. Grandma tried intermittently to reach over and offer to take the child from his mother. After several refusals, finally, Mom got so frustrated that she handed her baby over to Grandma.

Grandma obviously thought it best to take the baby out of the meeting, and rightly so, for many women kept looking over at the mom and baby, asking with their eyes if maybe there was something else she could do to quiet the baby. As Grandma got up abruptly, she grabbed the baby's blanket and walked to the side of the auditorium. Several of us sitting close by were taken aback by the way this grandma treated that baby. She handled the baby angrily and roughly and her irritation was evident to all of us. She held him awkwardly away from her body, probably so that her good clothes would not get soiled.

I watched as that little baby struggled being held that way, with his little legs dangling down, no socks or covering on the little mottled legs that were obviously cold. The blanket had been tucked through this grandma's purse strap in order to carry it, and it appeared that she did not think of it again. So the cuddly softness of the blanket that might have provided some comfort and warmth was not available to the child either. Cold room, cold grandma, cold experience, it seemed—what must that little one have thought of his world that day? He cried and fussed; no amount of Grandma's jiggling comforted him. All us moms sitting there with this situation in plain view seemed to want to intervene and ask the grandma if she needed help, but we all thought better of it. Soon Mom came to relieve Grandma. She at least wrapped the blanket around her little one, but she was awkward, rough, and angry with the baby, too. There was no warmth in her response to her baby and his needs, either. Might this little one eventually give up trying to have his needs be met and attach in an avoidant way?

Both the mom of the ambivalently attached child and the mom of the avoidantly attached child can give confusing messages in their responses. There is seldom, if ever, a healthy balance between tender and tough in these moms. Moms of ambivalently attached children are so unpredictable that their children cannot find any consistency in Mom's care. She at times is too tender and at other times too tough. Moms of avoidantly attached children tend to be tough, but their children usually do not experience Mom's toughness as loving limit setting, but as coldness or harshness.

The infants in both of these insecure attachment styles became fearful and developed an internal model of an unsafe world that affected them throughout life. It showed up as lowered self-worth and an inability to form healthy adult relationships. Ainsworth confirmed in her research that there is a particular way that a mom treats her child and that treatment dictates the way her child will attach to her. Later research showed that these patterns tend to persist into adulthood. But even the mom of the securely attached child can give messages that are confusing, as she may become permissive or react in anger out of frustration. Again, no mom can do it perfectly. The goal is to find out how to fill in the gaps of what we received so that our own children can get "enough" of both tender and tough.

What We Needed

So how do we define the tender, safe, warm, and nurturing response that our moms could have given that would have been best for us? Of course, in looking at descriptions of the care that each of us needed, it becomes a subjective evaluation as to how we experienced it and how much we needed. But there are some aspects of a mom's treatment that are basic. We can look at these basics in order to get an idea of what we all needed in the beginning. In the next chapters, we will identify some of these dimensions of tenderness as we experienced them from our moms. We will see in a later chapter how these are attributes demonstrated for us perfectly in God's character, traits that we know come from his tender heart. In God's relationship with us, his children, he shows us a perfect balanced treatment that is best.

We needed our "cups" filled to a capacity that Mom could not achieve perfectly. It was not just a matter of whether our mom had a personality bent that gave her the ability to be more tender or more tough, but also a matter of the influence that her past history provided for many dimensions and distortions of tenderness as well as of toughness. We will see that an absence of tenderness does not equal the right kind of toughness, just as an absence of toughness is not necessarily tenderness.

In the research Ainsworth did, in observing attachment patterns that infants were forming with their mothers, she identified several dimensions that described how a mom relates to her child. Here we will use some of those dimensions as a basis to describe the trait of tenderness and to see how they affect our ability to set loving limits. They are:

1.) *Availability*, how present and accessible our mom was
2.) *Responsiveness*, how sensitive our mom was to our signals
3.) *Acceptance*, how accepting our mom was of us and how well she was able to give us the limits we needed

In the next three chapters, we will describe each of these three dimensions of tenderness and help you evaluate your experience of how your own mother treated you as a child.

It is important that you keep in mind that we are not assigning a diagnosis of any kind to a mom by looking at these dimensions of tenderness. We are trying to get a picture of the way you may have formed your first impressions of the world and yourself, perceptions that may have influenced how you mother your own children. This is not a judgment on your mom, but a look at life from your perspective as a child. Dad also had a great influence on you during your growing-up years, but here we are looking mostly at a mom's influence, as she was usually there first and had the greatest influence.

Thoughts to Consider:
Babies attach either in a secure way or insecure way to Mom or a mother substitute, depending on her availability and on the responses she gave. If Mom was available when her baby needed her and gave warm responses that were in tune with her baby's needs, her baby could attach to her in a secure way. These attachment styles are carried into adulthood and affect how we relate as adults.

What do you think babies need most in their first months? Can you think of things other than what was mentioned in this chapter?

How do you think you attached to your mom, in a secure way or in an insecure way? Why do you think so?

A Mom's Prayer

Dear Heavenly Father,

As I look more closely at the specifics of how I experienced the treatment I received in childhood, help me to begin to understand more about what I brought with me into adulthood and how it affects me. When I feel discouraged about what I received or did not receive, help me to lean on your love and encouragement. I want to know more about your healing power and how you can fill in any gaps that were left in the care I received.

In the name of Jesus,
Amen

Chapter Six

We Longed for Mom's Presence

A young child's hunger for his mother's love and presence is as great as his hunger for food.

JOHN BOWLBY

From my seat I could see that my six-year-old grandson, David, was scanning the audience. In fact, all the kindergartners there on stage that evening were anxiously looking over the crowd of parents and relatives gathered for the Kindergarten Graduation. They had just marched into the auditorium to the music of "Pomp and Circumstance," and now were standing on the plat-form facing the audience. They were all dressed up—the little girls in their frilly dresses and lacy socks and the boys in their best clothes. David was, of course I thought, the most hand-some in the group, dressed in his little double-breasted navy blazer, white button-down shirt, and tie. I watched as each little student found a familiar face in the audience, gave a smile, and a little embarrassed wave, and then relaxed. David hadn't found us yet, and you could tell he was getting worried by the questioning frown on his face.

Then all of a sudden he caught sight of his family. A smile spread across his face and he relaxed. His family was there! Even more importantly, Mom was there!

The Dimension of Availability

In this chapter we will look more closely at one dimension of tenderness, a mom's availability—that is, how present she was in our lives when we were children. We saw how critical Mom's presence is in an infant's attachment process. And all through childhood and the teen years if Mom was available she provided the security we all needed at each stage of our development. She could have been a stay-at-home mom, or a working mom who arranged her work schedule to be available to her children, but if she was there, not just physically but emotionally, we could feel safe.

The mom who is available is open to her child, dependable and approachable. Her child experiences her as trustworthy, and feels protected as he senses her presence. She is able to hold and cuddle her child when he needs it and her closeness makes her child feel secure. The trust a child is developing is trust for Mom, as he learns he can count on her to be there when he needs her to be. And building on his trust of Mom, he is learning that the world may be safe, too.

The mom who is available to her child is there when needed, even present through tough, stressful circumstances. She is there even when she does not really feel like being there for a colicky baby or a cranky or sick toddler.

If our mom was available in good enough doses as we reached toddler age, we continued to build our trust in her and in the world. There was no fear in us as we came to Mom to have her kiss our "owie," or put a band-aid on it. She tenderly received us. If Mom was on the phone, temporarily distracted or busy elsewhere we didn't panic, for we knew that she was available, if needed, for anything that was serious. When we needed to sit on her lap and have her read to us, she was there. When we needed her to let us explore, she allowed it.

If Mom was available enough for us in childhood, we reap the benefits as adults.

> *Mom was available—I felt safe—I learned to trust.*

If Mom Was Not Available

But what if we had a mom who was not available, a mom who gave too little of herself when we needed her? Mom could have been ill, too tired, too busy, depressed, working too much, or just not interested in being available to her child. She could have been too preoccupied with her own life, or maybe living with stressful circumstances that kept her from giving what her child needed.

Moms who are unavailable do not fulfill their child's needs to have her presence so that he can make a secure attachment to her. Mom feels unsafe because she may be unpredictable and even scary. When a child's needs accelerate during an illness or night fears and Mom is not there to comfort him, he is left to fend for himself way too early. He learns that the world is not safe because no one comes when he has a need.

Pam, a mom who said that she would describe her mom as unavailable, told me that her mom started a new business when she was only a year old. She said that she has no memory of her mother except as a businesswoman dressed up in a suit. She remembers that her mom always left the house early, even before Pam and her brother were awake, and did not come home until after dinner. Dad was there in the mornings until the baby-sitter arrived, but Pam said that he was too tired from his own job to do anything with the kids. Dinner was mostly take-out food that Dad picked up on his way home from work. She and her brother had to entertain and raise themselves.

Pam says that she wishes that her mom could have been there for her but that she is OK as an adult and that she learned to not lean on anyone for much of anything. She says that she knows that her kids need more from her than she received, but that she really wants them to learn independence, too. At this time Pam has a nanny who keeps her kids full time.

Jamie, presently a mother of two teenagers, describes how she felt abandoned by her mom who was not there when she needed her:

As an only child, I had everything. My parents gave me all that I ever wanted or needed. If I saw something in the toy store, my mom always bought it. And she encouraged my dad to bring me something every time he came home from a trip. So you see, I had no need for anything material. Even when I became a teenager, they supplied all the clothes and shoes and anything that was the latest. Sometimes I got things that I didn't even want. I don't understand why they did that, except that it seemed that they tried hard to make me happy. I don't think my mom knew how to be a mother for she never showed me or told me that she loved me.

My mom and dad were always going off on trips and they never knew how insecure it felt to me when they would just take off. When I was very young, they, of course, got a sitter for me when they wanted to go, and they went a lot. But when I was about eleven or twelve, they just simply left me home alone. They knew that I was so well behaved and could take such good care of myself, that they had great confidence in me to be all right while they were gone. They would go off on weekend trips and not think a thing about whether I was lonely or not. At the time I felt like it was really cool that they trusted me so much, and I really enjoyed being there by myself, but now I know that it was not a good thing. It was not until recently that I had given any thought to the fact that I was so lonely as a child. A counselor once told me to think about it this way: When I see a child who is about the same age I was when they left me alone, would I think that that child was capable of being left alone? Then it really hits me and I get angry about it. What were they thinking? It was not physically safe for me to be left alone, and surely, it was not good for my own emotional development.

But Mom can do so many things well. She is amazing. Many of her friends are in awe of her. She has a design business and runs that besides a thousand other things. And now she can juggle all that and still see my kids, even though it seemed she never had time for me when I was little. But warmth and closeness, I will never get from her. Oh, how I longed as a kid for her to just hold me and cuddle me when I got my feelings hurt, but that almost never happened. My dad was there some and he did hold me at times, so I feel closer to him than Mom. But he was also so busy that he did not really fill in where I felt abandoned by Mom. I describe her (I would never tell her this) as a porcupine. She was never available to me. You can never get past her pricklies to get to the inside of her. She would probably never understand that I feel this way about her. She lives in her own world, and I circle on the outside and never really get close. I am happy that my kids get to have a tiny part of her, something that I never got to have.

I feel a bit sorry for my mom and yet I feel angry at her at the same time. She has not had such a wonderful life. I know that her own mom was very cold and distant and maybe even cruel to her. The stories I have heard about my grandma tell me she was a harsh lady. She was someone I never knew because she died when my mom was a teenager. My mom had to fend for herself, and maybe that's why she thought that I could take care of myself when she was gone so much. But she should not have ever left me alone when I was a child. I don't know if I can ever forgive her for that. I would never leave my child like that.

The Consequences of Having an Unavailable Mom

If Mom was not available enough for us in childhood, we as adults reap the consequences. We learned that it's not always good to trust. We think hurtful things might happen if one trusts too much. Abandonment issues are often central to our relationships. We take on a protective front, making sure that we don't feel abandoned again. We will protect ourselves either by shutting down our own needs or by projecting our needs on our children and caring too much for them. When we shut down, we typically fit the too-tough pattern, and when we project our needs, we become too tenderhearted.

Mom wasn't available—I felt lonely and abandoned— I learned that the world was not a safe place to be.

Did an unavailable mom raise you? If so, here are some things you may need to watch for in your relationships, especially the relationships with your children. These are some of the things that suggest you are either repeating the pattern of treatment you received or reacting against that pattern. Either way, you are not free to be the mom you want to be, and your struggle with finding the balance between tenderheartedness and tough-mindedness is intensified.

Some, like Jamie, who had moms who were not present enough, find that they have reacted and have made a concentrated effort to mother differently than they were mothered. They fall into a somewhat compulsive care-giver role. Instead of repeating the abandoning treatment they received from their mom, they give to their own children the tenderness and closeness they longed to have, and seek to avoid any sense of toughness in their mothering. They are determined to do it differently, and usually end up giving too much and being too tender.

If you are reacting to a mom who was unavailable, you may:

- Work too hard at keeping everyone else happy—so much so that there is no time for you to meet any of your own needs.
- Struggle with feelings of being abandoned. You find that you are always accommodating everyone else for fear they might judge you or reject you in some way.
- Find it is hard to get appropriately tough, but more often get angry and overreact in situations that call for toughness.
- Still try to get affirmation from your mom, especially when you see that she can give it to her grandchildren.
- Find that you still get angry at your mom's inattention to you. You may even experience feelings of depression and emptiness when you think about her.

Other adults who were raised by unavailable moms may have found that because showing needs made mom anxious or made her "go away," they shut off their own needy feelings and became "needless." They became very independent too early, learning to not lean on anyone. They may even rationalize that what they received was good enough for them and they often look on their childhood as adequate. They may end up like Pam—she is finding that she is repeating the same pattern with her children by staying too objective. Consequently her children may experience her as being unavailable to them.

Pam is an unavailable mom who was raised by an unavailable mom. She is the more typical adult child of this type of mom.

Most daughters raised by a mom who was not there for her children, either physically or emotionally, create the same pattern in the next generation. Pam's lack of a secure base in her childhood has led her to develop an independent sense of self-sufficiency that denies her own needs. If she is unable to even recognize her own needs as existing, it will be very difficult for her to have the resources to recognize and respond to the needs of her children. Instead of being too tender, moms like Pam come across as cold, withdrawn, or as being too tough.

If you are repeating your mom's pattern, you may:

- Be seen at times by others as harsh and/or sarcastic, or insensitive to the emotions of others around you. You may see this as simply being objective.
- Have a hard time showing tenderness, and can get too tough.
- Have trouble feeling connected to loved ones in your family. You may long for more closeness and intimacy in your relationships, but you also have the feeling that this longing is a sign of weakness. Or you may see that longing for closeness as being almost insatiable.
- Have a life filled with achievements, but may also find that you are on a performance treadmill. Some of your achievements don't bring the same sense of satisfaction they used to bring.
- Find that those who are dependent on you irritate you. You like it when you are independent and can set yourself on a track to reach a goal.
- Become verbally abusive to your mother, either through sarcasm or outright criticism.

If Mom Was Smothering

When there is too much availability on the part of the mother, she may come across as smothering. There is a lack of respect for her child's emotional space. The smothering mom needs to be there constantly and she must know everything. She is always in her child's face. The child gets way too much of Mom—more than is needed.

Some call the mom on this side of the continuum the "helicopter mom," a mom who constantly hovers over her children. However, some of these moms can also be very unpredictable in their care. They may be available and then all of a sudden get caught up in their own agenda and become unavailable. Their children experience this unpredictability as insecurity, and it may be the source of the ambivalently–anxious pattern of attachment as described earlier.

Sandy describes her smothering mom:

I am the oldest of three kids. My mom was right there with us kids every minute. I don't know how she did it. The good part is that she was there. But the bad part is that she has never let us go. She has lived her life through us kids and has never really found out who she is and has never gotten a life of her own. She is about the most insecure person that I know. The way she always puts herself down is really tough to live with. I understand that she has always needed to do everything for us kids—that's probably the one thing she does that helps her feel good about herself. But she also is one of the most helpful people that I know, even though others don't appreciate what she does at times. In a way it's pretty nice for us kids, as she is always giving us things, or bringing something over she has made, but we all want her to have a life besides us. I guess I notice it more than my brothers do, as the daughter. She is absolutely obsessed with the three of us. Sometimes she gets on my nerves. She is always saying that she is not good enough, and I want to say, "Mom, give it up." I don't know how my dad has put up with it.

I can't help but feel angry with her at times, and I do get frustrated and yell at her, and then she just gets her feelings hurt. But then she is right back at it. I want to act appreciative of all that she does, but honestly, she makes me crazy with all her fussing, and so I avoid her sometimes. Early on, I decided that I did not want to be like my mom. Instead, I really identified more with my dad. Mom did not seem like a very adequate person to me and I don't know where I got such thoughts so early, but I know that they were there. She was almost an embarrassment to me. I never wanted my friends to see how she was. But my friends never seemed to understand what my problem was with her. They said that they would have loved to have a mom like her who was always there to do things for you.

I don't have a lot of patience with people when they can't stand up for themselves, and Mom is really extreme. She just seems so dependent, weak, and inadequate to me. I have made sure that I did not become like her. Maybe I have gone to the opposite extreme, but I think that is the way I had to do it. I knew that if I did not, I would have been consumed by her like two of my brothers have been.

They do not have a life of their own at all. I get so disgusted with them, when they still cater to her and lean on her for money. I don't see how they stand themselves.

Eileen, a mom in her forties, feels she can't ever detach herself from her mom's control. She says that she is afraid to give up the benefits that go with not resisting her mom's overinvolvement in her life. For the first two years she was married, she and her husband lived with her mom. Both she and her husband gave their checks to her mom and she paid off their debts. Then Eileen's mom gave them the money for a down payment on a house and for furniture. Now she and her husband are in debt again, and Mom has offered to bail them out once again. Eileen resents her mom's control but says, "I don't know what else to do. I know that makes it easy for my mom to continue to control my life, but what else can I do?" Instead of working on other solutions to her money problems, Eileen pours herself into her own children. Part of why she's in financial trouble again is that she can't say "no" to anything her kids want. She's trapped in her own dependent relationship with her mother, but she's also repeating it with her own kids.

The Consequences of Having a Smothering Mom

If a smothering mom raised us and she was somewhat consistent in hovering over us as an infants, not a lot of harm is done. Remember, infants need the constancy of Mom's presence. But as we grew, a mom who continued to smother could have done harm as we tried to separate from her. And if she was unpredictable, going from smothering to being unavailable, we became watchful and anxious. By the time we become adults, such moms are often too much for us, and we struggle with a relationship with them that feels confining.

> *Mom was too available—I felt smothered—I struggled to learn who I was apart from Mom.*

Were you raised by a smothering mom? Look at how you react to your mom today. Do you get frustrated with her, seeing her as weak and needy and yet controlling? Do you find yourself getting angry with your mom, but unable to be clear and direct with her about what you are feeling? Do you sometimes wonder if you are too dependent on your mom, or that she is too dependent on you?

Sandy, who said she experienced her mom as smothering, described her mom's presence as anxious attempts that led her mom to often interfere in Sandy's life. While Sandy and her siblings were growing up, Mom was basically a very permissive mom (we'll look at this aspect later) who couldn't say "no" to her children. She still can't say no to her adult children, and she can't hear Sandy's "no" either. The boundaries between Sandy and her mom have been blurred and very unpredictable. Even now, in her late sixties, Sandy's mom is still very dependent and holds on tenaciously to her mothering role with her adult children. You can see that Sandy has tried not to repeat her mother's style, and tends to react against her mother's style and become almost too detached from her own children. Her fear of being like her mom has pushed her to the other side of the spectrum.

If you had a smothering mom, here are some things you might want to watch for in your relationships. You may be repeating you mom's pattern, or reacting against that pattern. Either way, you may struggle with finding the balance between tenderheartedness and tough-mindedness.

Some, like Sandy, in trying hard to mother differently, find themselves still reacting to their own moms, even though they are now adults. What they don't realize is that in reacting, mother is still in charge. She is still determining Sandy's behavior.

If you are reacting to a smothering mom, you may:

- Tend to feel overwhelmed, and have a difficult time getting your life organized. You tend to think you can do much more than is reasonable, but of course, you think it is reasonable to expect that of yourself.
- Have a hard time showing tenderness, instead try to show a tough front.
- Find yourself being angry with your mom and want to withdraw from any contact with her.
- Have developed a better relationship with your dad, and use him to filter your contact with your mom.
- Have a tendency to be self-sufficient, shutting off your need for others because you don't want to be like your mom.

Eileen, on the other hand, is still passive and dependent on her mom, even though she is now a mom with teenage children. Her boundaries are blurred, or non-existent. She lives in the shadow of her mom. And because she has failed to develop her own sense of self, she feels paralyzed. She is repeating her mom's style of mothering.

If you are repeating the smothering behavior of your mom, you may:

- Have a hard time saying "no" to your children, or to anyone else. Personal boundaries are very difficult for you to set and enforce.
- Find it easy to show tenderness and have trouble being tough when the situation calls for it.
- Worry that others are not as interested in getting to know you as you are in getting to know them.
- Struggle with your image of yourself. Even when someone gives you a compliment, you wonder why he or she is saying what they say. It's hard for you to accept that someone really likes you and admires something about you.
- Struggle with burning the candle at both ends. You work hard at meeting everyone else's needs, even to the point of neglecting your own health and welfare.
- Have feelings of depression on and off throughout your life. In addition, you may also have an undercurrent of anxiety that is always there under the surface.

Some children of smothering mothers like Eileen follow in their mother's footsteps. Others like Sandy react against their mother and develop a self-sufficient, tougher style. Either something in the personality make-up of the child, birth order, or in the child's relationships with other family members determines which path a mom will choose. For Sandy, her strong relationship with her father may have given her the impetus to follow a pattern of toughness to a fault. Eileen chose the other path and deals with her kids in an overly-tender way.

Whether Mom was unavailable, too available to us, or unpredictable in her availability during our childhood, we will deal with abandonment issues in relationships. Even if we knew that Mom was there, we also knew that she might abandon us if we did not fit into her agenda.

"Unavailable" and "smothering" are the two extremes of availability. What do you remember or what were you told about the availability of your mom when you were a child? Think on it for a minute and then put an "X" on the continuum between the two extremes, at a place that you think best describes how your mom responded to you on the dimension of availability. You will probably recall times when you felt as if mom was not there and other times when she felt smothering. But put a mark on the side to which your mom "leaned." What treatment do you think you received, mostly?

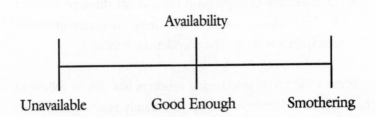

Availability

Unavailable   Good Enough   Smothering

Thoughts to Consider:

We learned to trust and felt secure if we found that we could count on Mom to be present and available to us when we needed her. If she was unavailable, we learned that the world was not a safe place to be. If she was too available, we felt smothered and had a hard time learning who we were as separate from Mom. Either way we found we would have to make adjustments in what we needed in order to protect ourselves from the pain of an insecure environment.

In reading the stories other moms told who described their own moms as unavailable or smothering, what did you identify with the most as you reflected on how you were treated as a child?

What do you remember about the presence of your mom in your home when you were young? Was she your primary care-giver when you were an infant? Was she usually there to welcome you when you came home from school?

(If you are having a difficult time thinking about where your mother was when you were little, consider asking a sibling, an aunt or your grandma or grandpa about what they remember about her presence when you were a child.)

Whom do you remember as the person who provided warmth and protection in your home when you were a child? Was it someone other than Mom? How did he or she make you feel warm and secure?

A Mom's Prayer

Dear Heavenly Father,

Looking at my past is not very comfortable for me. Will you guide me as I search for understanding about how the availability of my mom affected me? Where I do not feel safe and protected, help me to have confidence in your presence and the security that it brings. When I feel lonely, help me to sense your availability in a powerful way, even when I doubt that you are here with me. There are so many places that I may need you to fill me up with your presence. Will you increase my faith as I invite your presence into more and more areas of my life?

In the name of Jesus,
Amen

Chapter Seven

We Needed Mom's Tender Response

When Mom and child sing the same song, the music they make fills both their souls with sunshine.

JUDITH MCCLAREY

A couple of weeks ago when I went to pick up my little grandson, Jonathan, from nursery school, I noticed a little girl sitting on the picnic bench next to the playground, sobbing quietly. She looked to be about four years old or so and seemed to be so vulnerable and lonely there by herself. Now I know that I have a tendency to get involved where I shouldn't and so I thought, *Oh, there are several teachers here. Surely they have checked on her.* So I directed my attention elsewhere. But after several minutes had gone by I realized that no one had paid any attention to her. The teachers walked back and forth but never said a word to her.

That's it, someone needs to check on her, I thought. I went over very quietly and said to her, "Are you OK?"

"My friend poked me in the eye really hard," she seemed relieved to tell me.

I looked at her eye, all red and swollen, and said to the next teacher who walked by, "Do you think someone should look at this little girl's eye?"

121

"Oh," the teacher replied, "we've all talked to her. She's OK."

After a few minutes, as I waited for Jonathan to finish playing in the sandbox, I glanced over at the little girl again. A teacher standing near me sensed that I was still bothered, and leaned over and said to me, "I'm her teacher, and believe me, she's really OK. There's always something wrong with her. She's really a handful—requires a lot of my time."

Just then, another teacher came by and took the little girl by the hand to take her inside. As she walked by, she said, loudly enough for all of us standing nearby, including the little girl, to hear, "She's just a little melodramatic. She'll be OK."

OK? I thought as I got Jonathan's things and walked him to my car. I wondered what had given that little girl such a reputation. If she did demand a lot of attention, what could have made her need it so badly? How had her needs been responded to at home? It was obvious how she was being responded to here at preschool—at least today. How would her mom respond when told by her little one what had happened that day at school? Would her mom also dismiss her needs as coming from a little girl who was being just a little melodramatic? Did her teachers somehow think that they were helping her by using a kind of toughness with her? Would she begin to see herself as unaccepted and unloved and take the label with her throughout life, bearing the effects of it in all her relationships?

The Dimension of Responsiveness

Who really saw us as precious enough to be sensitive enough to respond to our needs? Every one of us as children wanted to have Mom be attuned to our needs so that we could relax in her presence and know that she could read our signals. We saw in the last chapter that if Mom was available, we were able to feel safe enough to begin to trust. Also basic to building that trust is the confidence that we are being understood. We wanted and expected Mom to be sensitive enough to our needs so that when we put out attaching behaviors we knew that there would be a positive response. If she ignored our signals or was insensitive to them, we felt confused and may have wondered what was wrong with us. If she over-reacted to our signals, she may have tried to meet a need that we did not have. Then we became frustrated and anxious as we tried harder to tell her what it was that we needed. For instance, maybe Mom tried to feed us when all we really wanted and needed was to be held.

Some moms are more able than others to give their child sensitive responses that continually say, "I care enough about you that I will make an effort to read your signals accurately and respond in a loving and tender manner." An experience I had on an airplane flight recently showed me close up how a mom can learn to read her child's signals.

I was thinking that I would catch up on my sleep on this trip, and I was delighted to find that the seat I had been assigned was right in the front of the plane at the bulkhead. I was just about to get settled when the man who had the seat next to me said, "Before you get your things put away, could I ask you for a

favor? My friend has a seat a few rows back, and I was wondering if you would change seats with him so we could sit together?"
Now, I remembered all the times when my husband and I had not gotten seats assigned together and had asked others to change with one of us. And they usually graciously agreed. So I took a look at the seat in the back and rationalized that it would probably be quieter back there anyway, as there would not be all the going back and forth to the rest rooms, which were right there in front of this seat. So I said, "I guess it would be all right."

I took my things and moved to the other seat and got settled with blanket and pillow ready. The seat next to me was empty. The plane was already mostly full and I thought, *Wouldn't it be nice if that seat remained empty so that I would not have to worry about whether another person would want to talk to me.*

At the last minute, two young women came trudging down the aisle, each carrying one of a set of twin baby boys in their arms and a bulging bag over her shoulder. One woman was also carrying a car seat and the other was leading along a little girl who looked to be about three years old or so. They were checking the seat numbers, and sure enough they had the two seats right in front of me and the one right next to me.

The one woman, the mom of all three of the children, took the seats in front of me and settled her toddler into his car seat and one baby in her lap. The other woman and one of the twins sat next to me. After much passing back and forth over the seats of blankets, toys, packets of crackers, and sippy cups, they got settled and we were ready to take off.

I was not proud of my thoughts. *See what I get for being nice to that man up front? After takeoff maybe I should go tell him that I have changed my mind. How could this happen when I am so tired?* I knew that I would not be able to stay objective and shut out this chaotic scene, let alone be able to sleep.

The one baby sitting beside me on his aunt's lap seemed content so far with all his toys and snacks. He had strikingly huge gray-blue eyes, and I knew that I would not be able to ignore him. Eventually when I commented on him, I also said that if I didn't seem very friendly, it was because I had not had any sleep the night before and that I was probably going to rest. The aunt smiled and responded that she hoped that she and the little boy would not bother me.

Well, of course, there was no opportunity for me to sleep, as I eventually joined in and helped by picking up dropped toys, asking the flight attendant for more juice and milk for the babies, and searching for packets of fish crackers lost down the side of the seat.

Not often do I get to observe a mom's responses to her young ones so intensely and for so long a period of time. Here was a mom who found herself in a situation that appeared extremely stressful, but she did what I thought not many moms in that situation could do. She gave each of her children positive sensitive responses throughout the whole five hours of the trip. She comforted each of them as she traded on and off one twin after the other with her sister sitting next to me. Each time one of the little boys was transferred back to Mom, the baby was met with a loving embrace and much smoothing of hair and gentle patting as she said, "You're OK, my precious. I'm right here. Are you hungry?" She sang to them, held them close and in between she reached over and gave loving pats to the three-year-old sitting next to her. How could a mom do it? She was obviously in love with her children and the sensitivity she showed in responding to their needs was evident. All three of her children had to know that they were important enough that Mom would hear them and respond in love. Mom showed them they were precious to her. I'm sure they were taking it in and forming internal models of themselves as loved, wanted human beings. I thought what a beautiful picture when Mom and child are in sync with each other.

Being responsive means that a mom is in sync with her child and is attuned and sensitive to what kind of response her child needs. It is the next step beyond being available. When her baby cries, the attuned mom not only goes to him, but also responds in a loving way to his specific needs. It is characteristic of the dance between a mother and child mentioned earlier. One signals and the other moves in response, each reading and responding to what the other is communicating to them.

> *Mom was responsive—I felt loved and precious—I learned my needs were valid.*

If Mom Was Not Appropriately Responsive

Some mothers are unresponsive and insensitive to what their children need. These are the mothers who are rather consistently experienced by their children as cold and uncaring and sometimes even cruel in their lack of responses. A milder example is the mother mentioned earlier, who held her child in the meeting but responded coldly to her child's need for cuddling. She responded but she was not sensitive enough to find out what her child really needed.

Rather than getting overly excited about a child's need, the unresponsive mother is always downplaying what her child needs, making molehills out of mountains. She is basically insensitive and even seems oblivious to her child's needs. If her child is crying, she routinely dismisses his cries, perhaps thinking that her child is just faking it in an effort to get attention. Or she may tell her child to stop crying, never checking to see what the problem might be. She often forces her child to eat when he is not hungry, or misreads the signal that her child is tired and needs to go to sleep. She may leave her child alone in the crib for long periods of time and put off feeding him or holding him.

The insecurely attached children, observed by Ainsworth, experienced the world as an unsafe or even hostile place to be because Mom did not respond appropriately. Either Mom was not able to, or somehow decided not to respond to her infant in a warm, sensitive, dependable way. A secure attachment requires that a mother respond to the needs of her children. She doesn't overrespond, nor does she ignore the needs of her child, but she is in tune with what her child needs.

Lori, a mother of three, tells about her mom, who she feels is an example of an unresponsive mom:

I had no real childhood. That's just the way it was. My mom never wanted kids and I wonder if she ever was in tune with my needs. I found that my mom was not going to respond to me from an early age. So I think somewhere along the line I quit expecting anything from her. My brother tells me that I cried and cried when I was a baby and that my mom just let me cry it out, day after day. My brother would try to give me a pacifier or bottle, but he could not calm me either. When you describe the insensitive mom, I think that's probably my mom. My needs were always dismissed. Our lives as children were always about Mom and Dad, never about us kids. I don't even think Mom thought about our needs. We were always sent to our room so that Mom and Dad could have their privacy and we were always spoken to in a mean, scolding way. We were never welcome in the room where they were talking.

Did I ever feel precious or valuable? No! Mom never hit me but I felt abused by her words. I knew that I was not wanted by the things she would say that really hurt me. I don't think she ever knew how badly the things she said hurt. She actually told me when I was a teenager that she had never wanted me.

I have tried at times to make up for all the years that I lost in not having a good relationship with her, but she does not respond much. She just has a way of letting me know that I don't mean anything to her. To this day, she is totally insensitive to what I am feeling. I will probably never know why that is. She seems to be so independent that she needs no one. She and my dad divorced when I was thirteen and he has never tried to contact me. I don't even know where he lives. I blame Mom for the loss of him in my life. I learned later that he was an alcoholic and had a hard time holding his own life together, but I would like to have him in my life. I want my kids to know who he is.

Now my mom treats my kids just like she treats me. I don't know how she does that. I feel very offended that my kids don't matter to her and it's like saying to me, I don't exist. It's amazing to me that she hasn't changed over the years. I want to say to her someday, "What gives? How come you can't even respond to my kids?"

Sue, another mom, told me that her mother was never responsive to her needs as a young child:

I remember as a young child crying in my room for long periods of time and neither Mom nor Dad ever came to see what was wrong. My older sister told me that when I was an infant, Mom never came when I cried in the night—my older sister was the one who had to get up and comfort me. Later on I found out that my mom was angry about having a second child and resented having to take care of me. My sister told me Mom would leave me in my crib for hours after I woke from a nap, rationalizing that I liked it there. Mom's response to me as the unwanted child was to ignore me. I experienced my mom as cold, insensitive, unresponsive, and uninterested. I have spent much of my adulthood struggling with how worthless I feel. Mostly I have trouble identifying my needs and I cannot communicate my needs to anyone even when I try. But I am now working on trying to see that my value was not set by my mom, but by a God who loves me and sees me as precious.

The Consequences of Having an Unresponsive Mom

If we had a mom who was unresponsive and insensitive to our needs, we may find that as adults we are in some way still searching for the response that we did not get from her. We try hard to get others' approval. Or, we may have found, like the second pattern of insecurely attached children Ainsworth described, that we decided early that if our needs were not met, we would shut down our needs. We learned to be unhealthily self-sufficient. Others of us learned that if we ignored our own needs and took care of Mom's needs, we could stay close to her. These are patterns we carry with us into adulthood.

Mom was unresponsive—I felt unloved and worthless—
I learned to devalue my needs.

If you had an insensitive, unresponsive mom, these are some of the things that suggest you may be repeating the same pattern, or reacting against that pattern. Either way, you will probably not be free to be the mom you want to be, and you will struggle with finding the balance between tenderheartedness and tough-mindedness.

Mothers like Lori are trying hard to reverse the pattern of

mothering that they received. They pay close attention to their children and are in danger of becoming overly involved and too tender with their children. At the same time, moms like Lori are still struggling with getting what they never received from their own mother. They may find it difficult to stay focused, sometimes working on their relationships with their own children, but then still being caught up in their own issues with their own mom.

If you are reacting against a mom who was unresponsive, you may:

- Feel you are unworthy in your relationships, often wondering why someone would want to be close to you.
- Have a negative outlook on other people. The same feelings you struggle with within yourself are the feelings you have towards others.
- Still expect mom to recognize and validate your needs and therefore set yourself up for more hurt.
- Try too hard to make relationships work, thinking that if you just said or did the right thing, others would respond warmly and positively to you.

Mothers like Sue have a hard time not repeating the mothering style that they received. Their own sense of self is so damaged that they do not believe that anyone, even their own children, really like and respect them. As a result, they hold back from all relationships for fear that they will be rejected. As a result, they simply repeat the pattern of unresponsiveness that was so painful to them as a child.

If you are repeating your mother's lack of responsiveness to you as a child, you may:

- Come across as too tough and even harsh or cold at times.
- Tend to write people off too quickly whenever there is a disagreement. You either assume you are wrong, or you fight too much to prove you are right.
- Hold back in your relationship with your husband, and maybe even with your children, for you have a deep fear that they will see you in a negative way.
- Have a difficult time identifying your own needs, feeling that it is wrong to even have such needs.

If Mom Is Intrusive

Moms who are too responsive are similar to the overly available moms, the "smothering" moms. They are the mothers who are constantly trying too hard to meet the needs of their child. These moms typically overreact to their child's needs, often making mountains out of molehills. They may be intrusive with their responses. They may be inappropriately sensitive to needs they imagine. Or they may be like the moms of the ambivalently-attached infants that Ainsworth described, who were very unpredictable in their responsiveness, responding warmly some-times and at other times dismissing their child's needs with cold and harsh treatment.

Carrie, a mother of a six-month-old, told me that when she was in first grade her mom was so overly sensitive to her needs that she would often visit her school and try to solve Carrie's problems, even minor misunderstandings with other children.

"I was embarrassed that my mom tried to constantly interfere," Carrie said. As a result, she learned not to tell her mom what went on at school for fear that her mom would overreact and respond inappropriately.

Carrie went on to say that her mom has continued to try too hard to "fix" things for her even now that she is an adult and mother herself. She says that she wishes she could tell her mom that she would enjoy being with her so much more if she would just relax and enjoy their time together rather than offering answers and help that Carrie does not want or need.

Another mom, Cynthia, also describes her mom as being on the intrusive side of the dimension of responsiveness.

My mom and I have been pretty close. I was an only child and I think my mom was really protective of me. I can understand it somewhat. It was as if she had all her eggs in one basket—me! She was strict and had lots of rules that were unbendable, and she was always checking on me to see how I was behaving. But I don't think there was much thought about what my needs really were. It was more like the rules were for her comfort rather than to teach me anything. If I did something wrong, there was never any discussion. It was just an arbitrary response to me based on the rules. At least that's how it felt to me.

It seems that the description of the intrusive mom fits her because she was always there in a controlling kind of way. She overresponded, and her responses always seemed to be misplaced. I can remember feeling very misunderstood and wanting my dad to sit down and talk with me in the evenings. But he never did. He only watched television and never gave me the time of day.

I have worked out some of the hurt I experienced and have come to understand my mom better. But I had not thought about how much she has influenced me in how I am mothering my own child. I can see already how demanding a child can be. I hope I can be sensitive to my daughter's needs without overpowering her, but sometimes it's hard.

The Consequences of Having an Intrusive Mom

If your mom was intrusive and responded to you in ways that made you feel angry or uncomfortable, you too will struggle with the value you place on your own needs. Moms who over-respond do not give us an accurate evaluation of our needs any more than the unresponsive mom does. Remember that we were looking to Mom to respond appropriately—to be attuned to our needs—so that what we deducted about our needs was that our needs were legitimate and that we were precious enough to her that she responded in a satisfying way.

---

*Mom was intrusive—I felt disrespected and controlled—
I learned to mistrust my needs.*

If you had an intrusive mom, these are some of the things that suggest you are either repeating the same pattern, or reacting against that pattern. Either way, it may be hard for you to be free to be the mom you want to be, and you may struggle with finding the balance between tenderheartedness and tough-mindedness in dealing with your own children.

Mothers like Carrie are trying hard to change the pattern of how they were mothered themselves. But when you have no model of healthy responsiveness, it is difficult to know how and when to respond to the needs of your own children without going to the opposite extreme and failing to respond appropriately.

If you are trying hard to be different from your intrusive mom, you may:

- Struggle with your own control issues, becoming very frustrated when your children or your husband don't do what they are supposed to be doing. Your attempts to control probably arise out of your own desire to not be controlled by others.
- Find you push away the very relationships you need and desire.
- Want to cut off any contact with your mom as a way to avoid feeling controlled.
- Find that you explode at your mom, or explode at the nearest person after talking with your mom.

If, like Cynthia, you are finding yourself repeating the intrusive pattern with your own children, you are also probably struggling with a lot of anger that never seems to get resolved. Often Dad is absent from the life of the family, so the intrusive mom invests all of her emotional energy into the children. When there is only one child, as in Cynthia's situation, that investment from Mom can be overwhelming.

If you are repeating the intrusive pattern of your mom, you may:

- Find it difficult to contain your own emotions, especially negative emotions. You are also frightened by other people's expressions of negative emotions.
- Find that you are repeating some of the same passive patterns of behavior you used to avoid Mom's control, only now you use it in relation to your husband and your children. These patterns of behavior may include such things as feeling sick to avoid feeling controlled, or other behaviors you used as a child.
- Struggle with an underlying depression, or find yourself expressing anger at the wrong person because you cannot get angry with your mom.
- Still work hard at getting your mother to validate you and your needs.

These are the two extremes of the dimension of responsiveness. How do you think your mom responded to you? Think on it for a minute and then put an "X" on the continuum between these two extremes, at a place that you think most typically describes how your mom responded to you on the dimension of responsiveness. Place your mark somewhere on either side of the center as you consider the side to which your mom "leaned."

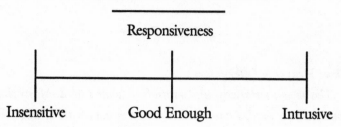

Thoughts to Consider:
A child learns how valued he is by how his needs are responded to. If he receives loving, tender responses that are appropriate to meet the needs he has, he sees himself as precious, valuable, and worthy of another's responses. If he does not get responses that are attuned to his needs, he feels misunderstood and sees himself as unloved and worthless, and he will devalue his own needs. If he experiences Mom as instrusive, he will feel controlled and disrespected.

What do you remember about your mom's ability to "be in sync" with your needs when you were a child? Did she try? Was she inappropriate many times?

Can you remember times when mom was "right-on" about a need, or even anticipated the need before you expressed it?

A Mom's Prayer

Dear Heavenly Father,

Thank you for always understanding what I need. Many times you know the needs I have even when I am not aware of what they are. And when I do acknowledge my need to you, you always respond to me. Help me to see myself as you see me, as valuable and precious. Others did not always give me responses that said that I was important to them. Will you help me to believe that you feel that I am "more precious than gold" to you?

In the name of Jesus,
Amen

Chapter Eight

We Needed Mom's Acceptance With Limits

I learn from you who I am.
Within your eyes I see
reflected me.
Within your voice I hear
how you see me.
You are the mirror that I look into
And mold the image of myself....

RUTH REARDON

As the fifth child born into my family, I grew up in a household with a lot of chaos and very few rules. Oh, there were some, like no dancing, and no going to movies, but other than that it was left up to me to decide what was right and what was wrong. There were lots of brothers and sisters to watch over me, and my mom was there to give me lots of appropriate loving responses. I knew that I was loved and that I was precious to her. But there was a downside. I had to set my own limits.

I can remember as a young child wondering why so many of my friends had parents who came to school functions to check on how their child was doing—I never had that. And there were those who had parents who came down hard on them because they didn't make the best grades. I watched them struggle with their parents' punishing, and sometimes rejecting, attitude. I thought, *How awful to have parents like that!* I knew I would never want that. At the time I thought it was great that no one was on my back about anything and no one checked to see if I did my homework or projects. Whatever I did in school was up to me. Whatever grades I made were fine with my mom. Whatever I decided, my mom said she trusted me.

My mom was sweet, tender, gentle, and accepting. But she was permissive. We kids knew that she struggled with feeling inadequate and lacked confidence in many areas. Back then we didn't think about what her own abusive background had to do with the way she mothered us.

Later, in looking at how having a permissive mom affected how tender or tough I would become as a mother, I realized that being on my own so early was not such a good thing. In fact it felt lonely to have no one providing the structure that could have given me the confidence that someone else was setting limits that would keep me contained. So in setting my own limits, I became very perfectionistic. I had to do everything just right. I had to make the very top grade in every class. Even when I put off projects until the last minute, I always somehow got it in and made sure it was over done. I tried hard to meet my own standards.

My mom accepted most everything. She never disapproved of any of my friends, male or female, and took a "hands off" attitude in most areas of raising me. I was treated with tenderness and gentle hands, but with no guidance about limits my confidence was eroded. I felt anxious and unsure of myself. I didn't know why. I didn't know that among the positive images

I was forming of myself because of a present and responsive mother, was another picture of myself as unconfident and inadequate—traits I saw in my mom. My mom did not know that I needed her to set limits for me so that I could feel sure about myself. Her "too accepting" attitude did not take into account my need for limits, a need that I did not even know I had.

In not understanding it, I repeated it.

So when it came to raising my own children, I made sure that I was available to them, that I responded to them with tenderness so that they would feel safe and precious. But I erred on the side of being too tender, not just because I am a more feeling-oriented person but because that was combined with what I learned from my own mom. I trusted my kids to do what was right. I never gave a thought to how that might feel to them. I had made it through with that type of mothering and so should my kids. I did not realize that they needed a lot more than my availability and responsiveness—that even with all the love I gave them, it was incomplete (we'll see later how God makes a mom's love complete). They needed more structure and boundaries than I gave them. They needed me to accept all their needs, including ones that included limits. It took me several years and a lot of stressful experiences to figure that out.

I saw myself as soft and tender and never internalized any view of myself as tough, too.

The Dimension of Acceptance

We saw earlier that if Mom is available, approachable, and there for us no matter what, we learn about safety and trust in relationships. If Mom is distant and unavailable, we feel unsafe and learn to not ask for what we need.

And we looked at how important it is for a mom to respond and be in tune with what her child's needs are. If she responds tenderly and appropriately her child begins to believe that his needs are valid. Those responses Mom gave provide a basis for him to feel valuable and even precious.

The third dimension that describes a mom's tender behavior is acceptance. As a child we wanted to see in her eyes and in her voice that we were accepted—that we were loved no matter what. We longed to see a response that showed us that she was in love with the whole of us. Then we could begin to feel confident and good about who we were.

But there is more to acceptance. As we grew we looked to Mom for the continued responses that showed her acceptance of us throughout our stages of development. As we moved out of the infant stage we needed not only her tender responses of acceptance, but needed her to set loving limits which gave us the structure we needed. Her acceptance that included a balance of loving limits profoundly affected how we went throughout life—causing us to learn about the lines between us and others. We began to learn that we were separate, individual human beings.

A mom's acceptance means that she accepted everything about our individuality. She may have had dreams of having a child with brown eyes and curly hair and we came with blue eyes and straight blond hair. She may have wanted a calm, malleable, sensitive child and got a wiry, resistant one. She may have wanted a boy and we came as female. A child who is accepted for who he is feels confident and learns to trust himself.

Acceptance means that Mom accepted us with all of our goodness and badness, all of our parts were accepted and all our needs were important. Acceptance also means that we were able to express our thoughts and feelings freely without fear of ridicule and criticism. But it did not mean that we could be free to do as we pleased, for that kind of permissiveness would have made us feel insecure and inadequate. If we had a mom who was less than accepting, we probably heard rejecting messages from her. If she was too accepting, like my mom was, we may have experienced her as permissive.

Some moms are more able than others to give their child appropriate accepting responses that continually say, "I love you. You are my child. I am pleased that you belong to me. I will love you no matter what and I will set the limits you need and give you the tenderness you deserve."

> *Mom accepted me—I felt loved and confident—I learned about limits set in the context of tenderness.*

If Mom Was Rejecting

What if we had a mom who was not able to give accepting messages and instead gave rejecting messages? Moms who are on the "too little" side, the rejecting side of this dimension, are characterized by a cold, unemotional, critical attitude. They give subtle, and sometimes overt, rejecting messages to their child that lead a child to doubt himself. If we as a child perceived that the looks our mom gave us said in some way, "I don't approve of you," we may have a hard time changing the way we view ourselves as we reach adulthood. Rejecting messages always undermine our confidence and are never the right kind of toughness that a child needs.

Criticism may have been commonplace in Mom's rejecting messages and eventually she may not have even realized she was doing it. The home atmosphere may have been one of strict rules, and when a rule was broken, we were made to feel guilty. In fact, guilt was almost constant, as we couldn't seem to do anything that got the approval of Mom. Often the rejecting mom tries to change this or that about her child to meet her own expectations. Mom may compare her child to other children, and may let her child know that he is not up to standard.

Amy, a mom of a teenage daughter, tells of how she experienced her mom as a rejecting mom:

From what I have learned since, I realize that my mom gave me rejecting messages. She had so many things that seemed so important to her. She always had to have the right outfit, the right shoes, and the right purse. She fussed and fussed over everything being just right. I never felt that I could live up to her standards. She always wanted to make sure that I was dressed perfectly and when we went out I had to behave exactly like she wanted me to. I think that it was part of the expectations of her generation that she and her friends were so aware of what other people thought. At times she would get so frustrated with my dad because he would say something like, "Oh, you look just fine. Let's just go." But my mom would throw up her hands and cry and tell him that he never understood the things that were important to her.

My mom had great expectations for me. She wanted me to go into the medical field in some way, and I know she is disappointed that I never became a professional woman. I have a cousin who seems to do everything in just the right way. As a child, anytime I did something wrong, my mom would say, "Would Christine do that? I don't think so." Christine could do no wrong in my mother's eyes. She is so pretty and always dresses so beautifully. Even when she was a little girl, she seemed to have a sense of style that my mom admired—a gift I certainly don't have. Mom would say to me, "Do you think Christine would wear that?" I learned to hate Christine. And of course, Christine went into nursing and now is a nurse practitioner. Even today Mom talks about Christine as if she was her own daughter.

Sometimes I want to scream at my mom and let her know how rejected I have felt, but I never do. It would do no good. I feel guilty about my feelings toward her at times. I know she is getting older and is coping with her own problems now. I don't think I will ever get her approval. I need to let it go, but it's hard.

Gretchen, a mother of two toddlers, also experienced her mom as rejecting her:

My mom was very young when she got married, I think, seventeen. She had my two brothers and my sister by the time she was twenty-five.

I remember feeling that us kids must have been so frustrating for Mom; she did not have much support from Dad and did not know anyone else in the town where we lived. But what I can remember most is that she was angry most of the time, and I don't know what she was angry about. Maybe it was because of her situation—she was so unhappy. I did not want to cause her any more stress and so I was always the "good" child. I went out of my way to help with my two brothers and my sister, and I always shielded Mom from having to deal with the little things that I thought I could take care of without asking her. But what I did never pleased her.

In the house we lived in during my years of about seven and eight, we had a great big window in the living room that had a wide ledge as the windowsill. I can remember sitting there for what seemed like hours, watching for my dad to come home. I looked out that window and imagined all kinds of ways that I might be rescued and taken to a family that would love me. As I look back on it I know that when I sat there I was feeling totally rejected, and unloved. I have a lot of sadness about that.

I know that now I am a totally caring, tenderhearted mother. I have a hard time sticking to the boundaries I set with my kids, but they are really good kids. I knew that I would never be like my mom. I probably have reacted and gone to the opposite extreme in taking too much responsibility for caring for others than I should, but sometimes I feel as if I go into withdrawal if I don't have someone to take care of. It's not that I feel I have to be the caretaker, but I really enjoy it—I really do!

The Consequences of Having a Rejecting Mom

Rejection can take the form of cutting a child off and just ignoring him. In the last chapter, if you realized that you had an unavailable mom, she was probably also a rejecting mom. These moms deny any kind of attaching behaviors by their child. If their child reaches for them, or cries to be held, the child's attaching behavior is dismissed and the child is seen as either spoiled or insecure. As a result, their child receives the rejecting message. This is a devastating kind of rejection. To be shut out or ignored results in a child's questioning his own reality.

Pia Mellody, in her book *Facing Codependence*,[1] writes of the underlying difficulties that result in codependency. She lists the difficulties in exercising appropriate levels of positive self-image and the inability to own and express our own reality as two of the basic difficulties she has observed in those dealing with codependency. Both of these can come as the result of rejection in childhood.

Mellody writes that these difficulties are based on not knowing who we are. She says that to know ourselves we have to be able to be aware of our own reality. Children who do not know or trust their own reality have been rejected in some way by being ignored, attacked, or abandoned for expressing what they perceived as reality. They learn it is not safe or appropriate to express what they feel or think or to trust how they act. For example, a mom who ignores her child's cries or tells her child that she can't stand him when he cries rejects him for having a need. Or the mom who threatens her child that if he continues to cry she will go crazy and leave him is terribly rejecting. Her child feels that it is his fault that mom is so upset and he begins to reevaluate whether what he feels or thinks comes from a real need.

Pia Mellody goes on to say that for children to have their reality denied is the worst experience a child can have. She gives the example of a little girl who came out of her room to find that Mom and Dad were having a terrible fight. Mom tells her little girl to go back into her room, that they are just having a disagreement and it is not horrible. Later when her daughter expresses distress about the fight, Mom tells her daughter, "Daddy didn't really say or do those things. You just thought he did." As a result, the child thinks she is crazy because her reality is denied.

If our reality was denied as children we lost confidence in our perception and we eventually stopped expressing what we felt or thought.

> *Mom rejected me—I felt unloved and unsure—I learned to question what I felt and thought.*

Amy, who earlier described her mom as rejecting, says that she finds that she catches herself saying things to her teenage daughter that sound just like her mom. Amy struggles with her self-confidence and sets up rigid standards for herself, somewhat like I did in dealing with my mom's permissiveness. But in contrast to my repeating a too tender attitude, Amy finds she is repeating her mom's tough, rejecting style of mothering. She says that she knows that she is very hard on her daughter and says things that she later regrets. She says that her husband thinks she is too strict and sometimes gives her daughter messages that hurt deeply. She worries that she is being swept along on a path that will lead her into the same relationship with her daughter that she had with her mom. She is beginning to see that understanding it and bringing it before the Lord will be healing and freeing for her.

If you find yourself repeating the behaviors of a rejecting mom, you may:

- Struggle against feeling powerless in relationships.
- Find that you have a lot of anger inside that you cannot understand.
- Develop a tough exterior to keep from being hurt by others.
- Find you have a hard time treating others with tenderness.
- Have high expectations for others and find you are often disappointed in them.
- Struggle with perfectionistic standards for yourself.
- Have a hard time setting appropriate boundaries.

Gretchen, the mom who has two toddlers, is trying hard to not repeat what she received from her mom, but finds herself being permissive and too tender. She has a hard time expressing

what she feels or thinks about anything. She has difficulty in setting limits for her children and instead defers to her husband if
anything needs to be dealt with. Gretchen's relationship pattern
with her mother always put her in the caregiving role. Gretchen
admits that she never allows herself to be the recipient of the
same kind of care she gives. Neither her husband nor children
know how to give nurturing care to her, as she gets uncomfortable when they try. Gretchen is an example of someone
raised by a mother who was unable to care for her and who instead
welcomed being cared for. Gretchen filled the role perfectly.

If you find yourself reacting to a rejecting mom you may:

- Work hard to keep the others in your family happy and
  strive to keep them from feeling any disappointments.
- Find you have difficulty in taking a strong stand with oth-
  ers for fear of rejection.
- Live with a lot of hidden shame.
- Keep people at a distance because you are afraid to be
  known by others.
- Tend to blame others for your inability to reach fulfillment
  in life.
- Struggle with perfectionism and high expectations.

If Mom Was Permissive

Moms who are on the "too much" side of acceptance are characterized by a permissive attitude that says anything goes—there
are no limits for the child. She may put her child on a pedestal
and then act as if the child can do no wrong. When her child
does something inappropriate all she does is smile and say, "Isn't

that cute!" Her child does not learn appropriate boundaries for his behavior.

Or it may be the mom who has an attitude that says, "whatever" in a flippant way of dismissing herself of the responsibility for setting limits—she can't be bothered with it. Or it may be the mom, like my mom, who is so sweet and loving that she takes a "hands off" attitude because she thinks being tough is mean. She seriously rationalizes that she does not need to have limits because she trusts her child so much. Either way, moms who are permissive give their child a feeling that he is on his own. He eventually feels insecure in making decisions that he is not mature enough to make.

A great many moms who describe themselves as too tenderhearted are really permissive. Permissive moms do not realize that a child does not experience permissiveness as tenderness or loving care. Rather a child usually experiences it as lack of caring and even as abandonment.

Jennifer, a mother of three, describes her mom as being on the permissive side:

While growing up I really took the fact that my mom never set any limits for me as normal. My mom had her hands full dealing with my dad. Dad was an alcoholic, but I never knew that when I was little. I just knew that he was sick a lot, and Mom never told any of us kids what the problem was. I can remember so many times seeing my mom sit outside on the steps with such a sad look on her face. It was only later when he got really bad that I found out about Dad.

My mom always let me do just about anything that I wanted. She is a very sweet person and very loving to me. She always had to worry about where she was going to get enough money to pay the rent and to get food. Even though she had it so hard, she never took it out on me. I always felt a lot of empathy for her. I think that I was such a good kid because I did not want to cause her any more worry. Mom had been raised by her grandma and I think that she must have been raised about the same way as she raised me, just because of the fact that her grandma was older and unable to be involved in my mom's life. My mom's mother died when she was about four years old, and I know her life had been really hard. She had to go to work when she was very young and she did not have a chance to go to college or get trained for a good job. I know she loves me and tried to do the best she could.

Margaret describes her mom as extremely permissive.

I don't want to say anything bad about my mom, but I am realizing how difficult it was for me to be raised without any rules at all. I have had a lot of problems with depression in my life, but my mom did, too. My mom had a hard time raising me and my brothers all by herself. My mom and dad were not divorced, but my dad was a traveling evangelist and was never home. It seemed that my mom had a lot of resentment about that. He would come home for a short time and when he was home I would hear them arguing in their room. I think it was over his traveling and about his not being there for our family. Mom always said that when he came home he would deal with my brothers and their misbehavior, but he never did. I was always somewhat in fear of him and when he lost his temper we all hurried to our rooms. He never hit me but I have seen him strike out at my brothers when he was really angry.

I think Mom wanted to make up to us kids for not having Dad there. So she was very soft and permissive with us. I can't say that she ever got angry or struck out at us. I was the good kid and my brothers took advantage of her softness. All three of us are still very close to Mom and we each in our own way appreciate the love she gave us. If she was too permissive, I can forgive her for it. I certainly understand why she was that way.

The Consequences of Having a Permissive Mom

To be accepted without any guidance or limits can leave a child feeling anxious and unsure of himself. Confidence not only comes from being accepted, but from the loving limits that a mom sets for her child.

Jennifer, the mother of three who described her mom as permissive, says, "I truly love my kids and want the very best for them. I know I come across as very soft and tenderhearted and I think it is mostly just the way I am made—I come out on the feeling side as far as my personality is concerned. But I can see that my mom's influence had a great impact on me, too. I had never thought about how much I find myself repeating the "hands off" style of mothering that she had with me. I am so surprised that you say that my kids may experience that as something other than my deep love for them. That scares me. I want my kids to have a balance in their lives and I want to understand how I am repeating my mom's style so that I can do it differently. My kids are still young and I feel that I am ready and willing to look at what needs to be healed in me so that I can give them what they need."

If you had a permissive mom and, like me, find that you are repeating her style you may:

- Find that you struggle with confidence in yourself to accomplish the goals you set.
- Are unable to stick by the limits you do set up.
- Are perfectionistic and set up impossible standards for yourself and others.
- Feel inadequate and try hard to hide that feeling from other people.
- Struggle with depression at times in your life.
- Have a hard time setting appropriate boundaries.

Margaret, who is reacting to her permissive mom, says, "I am raising my own kids with more restrictions than I had. I think that my husband has a lot to do with that. He is very definite in what he expects of them and he has helped me see that they really need limits to feel loved. I can feel that I am angrier at times than I should be and want to be able to deal with that in my life. I overreact to little things my kids do and then I am way too harsh and say hurtful things to them. My husband is trying to help me with that, but at times when he calls me on it I just get angrier. I get very discouraged when I can't stop and back down once I get angry. I know that my kids are going to suffer because of it.

I think I am probably reacting to my mom in some way but when I try to get stronger with my kids it has disastrous results. I need help!"

If you had a mom who was permissive and you are reacting to her style you may:

- Find that you have anger that stays hidden most of the time but that it comes out when you least expect it.
- Struggle with lack of confidence and feel inadequate most of the time in making decisions.
- React out of proportion to things that seem less important later.
- Set up standards for yourself that are perfectionistic and impossible to meet.
- Feel a lot of disappointment in yourself and your family when failure is obvious.
- Struggle with anxiety attacks or depression.
- Have a hard time setting appropriate boundaries.

Mom was permissive—I felt inadequate and anxious—
I struggled to set my own limits.

These are the two extremes of the dimension of acceptance: on one hand, the lack of acceptance experienced as rejection, on the other hand, inappropriate acceptance experienced as permissiveness. Think about them for a minute and then put an

"X" on the continuum at a place that you think most typically describes how your mom responded to you on the dimension of acceptance. Place your mark somewhere on either side as you consider the side to which your mom "leaned."

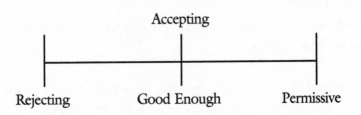

In the next chapter we will look at how God, our heavenly Father, wants to show us by his relationship with us as his children, what perfect tender love and perfect tough loving care look like. We will see how he wants to come into our lives and fill the places where there were losses and make us feel safe and precious. We will also see how he accepts us as we are with our needs for unconditional love and with needs for loving limits. Both come from his tender heart.

Thoughts to Consider:
A child learns who he is by seeing himself mirrored in his mom's accepting responses. If he receives warm, tender, "good enough" responses, he sees himself as acceptable and lovable and he learns to be confident. If he receives rejecting or critical responses, he sees himself as unlovable and will lack confidence in himself. If he is dealt a very permissive treatment, he becomes anxious and feels inadequate as he struggles to set his own limits.

If you received rejecting messages as a child, what do you think you could do to change those negative messages and the resulting images you formed of yourself?

How do you think having a permissive mom affects how you view tenderness and toughness in mothering? If you had a permissive mom, what kind of messages do you think you received about who you are?

A Mom's Prayer

Dear Heavenly Father,

Thank you for being the personal God who always accepts me as I am, and thank you for setting the limits that help me to follow your plan. Will you help me to see myself more as you see me? Others did not always give me responses that said that I was loved, no matter what. And sometimes others did not set loving limits for me so that I saw myself as confident and adequate. Will you correct those images that are inaccurate and give me the courage and ability to see myself mirrored in your response to me?

In the name of Jesus,
Amen

Part Four

Finding Strength in the Tender Heart

Chapter Nine

God's Provision for What We Needed

*The Lord is like a father to his children, tender
and compassionate to those who fear him. For he
understands how weak we are; he knows we are
only dust.*

PSALM 103:13-14

God wants us to see that he is all sufficient to fill in any place where we may have suffered a loss in what we received as a child. God is not only good enough in his tender care of us, but unlike any of our earthly parents, he is the perfect parent.

In my own life, when things seem to be the darkest and I need God's tender response, I often pray, "Heavenly Father, will you let me see a glimpse of your hand at work in this situation? I don't need to know the whole answer right now, and I trust you to choose when to show me more, but from my human viewpoint things seem so hopeless. Right now I just need to see that you are there working behind the scenes."

I have asked God many times for this kind of confirmation of his activity in my life. I can testify to the fact that he responds to my cry for reassurance of his presence. Like a loving parent, he hears my request and answers. It may be in the smallest tiny detail that he allows me to see his hand at work, but it confirms that he is there. That gives me hope when I need it most. Yes,

I have the reassurance from Scripture and from the history of God's activity in my life that he has not abandoned me. But at that very moment when I need some extra comforting reassurance, he is there, letting me know once again he is available when I need him. Just as a child, whose life has just seemed to fall apart, needs a comforting word of reassurance from his mom or dad that they are there, waiting for him to return to safety, God waits patiently for me to call on him for help. A secure child knows beyond a shadow of a doubt that his loving parent will be available for him; he can count on it. So it is with God and me. He is my secure base; I can count on him, for he never fails to be available to comfort me with his presence.

And in responding to my anguished cry, God never dismisses my need, whatever it is. He is perfectly in tune with every shade and intensity of any need that I bring to him. Because of God's tender response I know that my needs are valid and that I am precious to him.

Through God's acceptance of me, I learn more about his kind of love. He accepts me as I am and with all that I bring to him, with no condemnation. He never rejects me, yet he is never permissive. He allows me to face consequences because he loves me so much. He creates for me the boundaries that make me feel contained and confident in his all-encompassing love. He is perfectly tender with me—that never changes. When I experience his toughness and limits they are always in the context of his tenderness.

God's Wisdom in Our Creation

God planned that we would be brought into this world as tiny, vulnerable, helpless infants, totally dependent on a mother and father to meet our needs. Author Floyd McClung, in his book *The Father Heart of God*,[1] points out that God could have devised a reproductive system that produced ready-made adults. Instead he chose to create us as dependent babies who need a mom and dad. For it is in the setting of family that God intended for his love to be modeled. He wanted us to grow up accepted, loved, and understood. McClung describes God as the "perfect parent," who is faithful, generous, kind, and just, one who longs to spend time with his child. God wanted the family to be the nurturing environment within which we could develop so that as adults we would be ready and able to better understand his love for us. Throughout Scripture we see pictures of God that show us what a mother and father were to be like so that they could model his love.

The Tenderness of God

In her children's book, *God Is Like a Mother Hen*,[2] Carolyn Stahl Bohler uses metaphors that children can easily understand. She says, "God is like a mother hen who protects her little chicks." She bases this on Matthew 23:37, which says, "How often I have wanted to gather your children together as a hen protects her chicks beneath her wings...." Her words accompany a picture of a mother hen covering her baby chicks with her wings. She uses this, as well as other metaphors, to show a child what God is like, hastening to add that he is much, much more than any of these examples. I love the hen picture of God. I helps remind me that he is a loving, gentle, tenderhearted God much like a mother who wants to be with her children to protect them.

Author Richard Foster wrote, "His heart is the most sensitive and tender of all. No act goes unnoticed no matter how insignificant or small."[3] It is God's tenderness that draws us to him. And since he is a relational God who desires relationship with us, his creation, our Heavenly Father models for us throughout his Word the characteristics of a loving relationship. We see many pictures of his tender love for us. He is both the perfect father and the perfect mother figure. Everything that is good is found in the way he relates to us as his children. As David says in Psalm 103, "The LORD is like a father to his children, tender and compassionate to those who fear him" (Ps 103:13).

God wants to let us know that his love can fill in gaps due to deficient care we received from our very human mothers. I trust that in looking at the Scripture passages in this chapter you will find hope and confidence that no matter what residue from hurtful childhood experiences you may have carried into adulthood, God is waiting to fill you with the good things a perfect parent can provide. I know it to be true.

As we look at how God fulfills each dimension of tenderness, think about the places of emptiness that you might need God to fill. I have found that he wants to give to us in good measure, even giving until our cups are overflowing with his blessings (see Ps 23:5b).

The Dimension of Availability

> *God is always available—I feel safe—I learn that I can always trust him*

Unlike earthly parents, God is always perfectly available to us. He never abandons us or closes himself off from us. If we learned early on that the world was not a safe place because someone let us down, God is inviting us to trust that we are safe with him. Jeremiah wrote this great truth in the midst of his despair and disappointment at the fall of Jerusalem: "The unfailing love of the Lord never ends! By his mercies we have been kept from complete destruction. Great is his faithfulness; his mercies begin afresh each day" (Lam 3:22-23). He is always there when we need him.

God lets us know that even when we sleep, he is there watching over us. Psalmist David writes, "I will lie down in peace and sleep, for you alone, O Lord, will keep me safe" (Ps 4:8). God will never let us down, for as Paul wrote, "Even when we are too weak to have any faith left, he remains faithful to us ... and he will always carry out his promises to us" (2 Tm 2:13, TLB).

David wrote, "Listen closely to my prayer, O Lord; hear my urgent cry. I will call to you whenever trouble strikes, and you will answer me" (Ps 86:6-7). David anticipated the words of the writer of Hebrews, who said, "This High Priest of ours understands our weaknesses, for he faced all of the same temptations we do, yet he did not sin. So let us come boldly to the throne of our gracious God. There we will receive his mercy, and he will find grace to help us when we need it" (Heb 4:15-16). We can come to him anytime we have a need, no matter how big or how small. He never smothers us, but is available and waits patiently for us to come to him.

The Dimension of Responsiveness

> *God is responsive to my needs—I feel treasured—I learn that my needs are important to him.*

Responsiveness is key to a loving relationship. If we learned early that our needs were dismissed or misunderstood, God wants us to understand that his responsiveness is always right on target. He doesn't overrespond, nor does he ignore our needs. But he is sensitive and responds consistently and appropriately to our obvious needs and to the ones we don't even know about.

Author and speaker Elisabeth Elliot said, "The God who created, names and numbers the stars in the heavens, also numbers the hairs of my head.... He pays attention to very big things and to very small ones. What matters to me matters to Him, and that changes my life." That's the picture of God as parent who cares enough to be concerned with every detail of our lives and by that we know that we matter immensely to him. He values us enough to respond to us.

Paul expresses the wonder of a God who not only loves us in the details but is our resource for the kind of comforting responses we need to develop into whole persons. He wrote, "What a wonderful God we have—he is ... the source of every mercy, and the one who so wonderfully comforts and strengthens us" (2 Cor 1:3-4, TLB).

Notice how God reveals himself to us in "mothering" and "fathering" language. He is modeling for us the response that underlies unconditional love. I have already cited in chapter one a favorite verse that is written in mothering language. The prophet Zephaniah gives us an image of a God who loves us so much that he calms our hearts when we are afraid by singing to us, as a mother would sing to her child, lulling him into a peaceful sleep (see Zep 3:17).

In other passages we see pictures of God's responsiveness. Like a mother, Isaiah wrote, "I [God] will comfort you there as a child is comforted by its mother" (Is 66:13). In addition, God thinks about us and our needs constantly. Peter wrote, "Give all your worries and cares to God, for he cares about what happens to you" (1 Pt 5:7). And David wrote, "I will give repeated thanks to the Lord, praising him to everyone. For he stands beside the needy, ready to save them from those who condemn them" (Ps 109:30-31).

God shows us his tender responsiveness through Isaiah's words; "He will feed his flock like a shepherd. He will carry the lambs in his arms, holding them close to his heart. He will gently lead the mother sheep with their young" (Is 40:11). Like the perfect parent, God treasures us enough to meet our needs. Isaiah again pointed this out when he wrote, "The Lord will hold you in his hands for all to see—a splendid crown in the hands of God" (Is 62:3). He values us. He shows us off as a treasure.

In God's relationship with us he is always sensitive to what our needs are and responds exactly in a way that meets those needs. By the way he responds to us we know that we are precious to him.

The Dimension of Acceptance

God's acceptance of us is clearly shown in Romans 5, when Paul writes,

> When we were utterly helpless, Christ came at just the right time and died for us sinners. Now, no one is likely to die for a good person, though someone might be willing to die for a person who is especially good. But God showed his great love for us by sending Christ to die for us while we were still sinners.... For since we were restored to friendship with God by the death of his Son while we were still his enemies, we will certainly be delivered from eternal punishment by his life. So now we can rejoice in our wonderful new relationship with God—all because of what our Lord Jesus Christ has done for us in making us friends of God.
>
> ROMANS 5:6-8, 10-12

Notice the words Paul uses to describe us—we are "sinners," "helpless," and God's "enemies." And even in that state, God accepts us as we are and loves us so much that he willingly gave his Son to die for us, so we could be "friends of God." What a complete acceptance that is! If we felt rejected as a child, God wants us to see that by his loving acceptance he will fill up the parts left empty by rejection. He wants us to feel confident because he loves us as we are.

David writes, "My heart is confident in you, O God; no wonder I can sing your praises!" (Ps 108:1). And in Psalm 89:1-2, he says, "I will sing of the tender mercies of the Lord forever! Young and old will hear of your faithfulness. Your unfailing love will last forever. Your faithfulness is as enduring as the heavens." And in one of his most beautiful psalms, David writes, "He has not punished us for all our sins, nor does he deal with us as we deserve. For his unfailing love toward those who fear him is as great as the height of the heavens above the earth" (Ps 103:10-11). These words provide the foundation for what Paul writes in Romans 5. God accepts us in love!

God's Toughness in His Acceptance

God accepts me—I feel confident—I learn that the limits he sets are because of his love for me.

God's acceptance and love for us never lead to his being permissive. Paul responds to this idea in Romans 6, where he asks, "Well then, should we keep on sinning so that God can show us more and more kindness and forgiveness?" His answer is as strong as he can possibly make it. He says, "Of course not!" The tough side of God lets us know that there are limits. We encounter this in the beginning of God's relationship with mankind. In Genesis 3, Adam and Eve disobeyed God's instructions regarding one of the trees in the midst of the Garden. When he confronted Adam and Eve, we see tenderness in God in that he provides a promise of a solution for the problem of sin. But God also shows his toughness in that Adam and Eve are faced with the consequences of their sin. Eve is told that she "will bear children with intense pain and suffering" (Gn 3:16) and God told Adam that he had "placed a curse on the ground. All your life you will struggle to scratch a living from it. It will grow thorns and thistles for you, though you will eat of its grains" (Gn 3:17-18). Then he expelled Adam and Eve from the Garden. And "after banishing them from the garden, the Lord God stationed mighty angelic beings to the east of Eden. And a flaming sword flashed back and forth, guarding the way to the tree of life" (Gn 3:24). There were consequences for their actions!

The story of King Saul provides another example of God responding with toughness. In 1 Samuel 15, Saul was given a very specific task to perform. Samuel, the prophet, had been very explicit in his instructions to Saul—the Amalekites were to be totally destroyed. But Saul only obeyed partially. Because of Saul's disobedience, "the Lord said to Samuel, 'I am sorry that I ever made Saul king, for he has not been loyal to me and has again refused to obey me'" (1 Sm 15:10).

When Samuel confronted Saul, Saul offered his excuses. He spiritualized his disobedience, saying the sheep and cattle were salvaged in order "to sacrifice to the Lord your God" (verse 21). It is here that Samuel makes his firm, tough statement to Saul: "What is more pleasing to the Lord: your burnt offerings and sacrifices or your obedience to his voice? Obedience is far better than sacrifice. Listening to him is much better than offering the fat of rams. Rebellion is as bad as the sin of witchcraft, and stubbornness is as bad as worshiping idols. So because you have rejected the word of the Lord, he has rejected you from being king" (verses 22-23). Because Saul, as the leader of Israel, failed to obey, God dealt with him with toughness.

There are numerous other examples of God's toughness. God brings consequences to bear on mankind in the account of the Flood (see Gn 6–8), and again in the account of the Tower of Babel (see Gn 11). This side of God's character may bother some of us, but it is there for a purpose, which the writer of Hebrews, quoting from Proverbs 3:11-12, clearly explains. He writes, "My child, don't ignore it when the Lord disciplines you, and don't be discouraged when he corrects you. For the Lord disciplines those he loves, and he punishes those he accepts as his children" (Heb 12:5-6). Here we see the blending of tender and tough—God disciplines because he loves. The writer adds, "For our earthly fathers disciplined us for a few years, doing the best they knew how. But God's discipline is always right and good for us because it means we will share in his holiness. No discipline is enjoyable while it is happening—it is painful! But afterward there will be a quiet harvest of right living for those who are trained in this way" (Heb 12:10-11).

In this last passage, we can see the importance of the balance of tenderness with appropriate toughness. While it is painful in the moment, it leads to the fruit of "right living." Whenever

God uses his toughness, he is taking a stand. That stand is designed to precipitate a crisis. When Adam and Eve were expelled from the Garden, a crisis occurred—their life was radically changed. God's intention was that they might learn from the experience. When Saul was rejected by God as king, a crisis arose in the nation that wasn't resolved until David became king. Anytime God is tough with his children it is because he wants them to learn something.

Because God loves us, he responds to us with just the right balance of tenderness and toughness. He wants us to experience all of him, not just a part of him. A.W. Tozer wrote, "An infinite God can give all of Himself to each of His children. He does not distribute Himself that each may have a part, but to each one He gives all of Himself."[4] Through God's incredible love relationship with us, he gives us a picture of all it is that he intended a child to experience.

He waits for us to invite him to fill us with all of himself. That has been his intent ever since the beginning of creation.

How do we let God fill in the places where we need him most? Let's look in the next chapter at some steps that will prepare us for God's healing process.

Thoughts to Consider:

God wants not only to show us what he intended for us to have from our earthly moms, but he also wants us to experience the fulfillment of his love in all its facets. He is always available to us, responds lovingly to our needs, and accepts us as part of his unique creation. His acceptance is never permissive as he sets limits on our behavior because he cares so deeply about us.

As you've looked at some of the tender ways God cares about you, what new insights into how much he loves you did you discover?

When you consider where there were gaps in how you were mothered, do you believe God intends to fill in those places? How might he do that?

A Mom's Prayer

Dear Heavenly Father,

When I consider how you are like a parent who gives security and comfort to me as your child, I am awed. I love the wonderful ways you have of filling places where there may have been gaps in my care. Help me to see how your provision of loving care includes all that I ever needed in the way of tender or tough treatment. Thank you for giving me that message clearly in your Word and for the privilege of being your child.

In the name of Jesus,
Amen

Chapter Ten

Making Peace With What We Received

The problem we have as parents, then, is not usually a lack of love or good intentions, but more often an unwillingness to face who we are.
ROBERT KAREN, PH.D.

I have in my bedroom a not very attractive, old rocking chair. That is, it is not very attractive to those who do not know its history. It is spindly, not very sturdy at all, with many layers of black paint now worn through to the bare wood on all the edges. The seat should have been recovered years ago—the antique green fabric is now frayed and faded. But there it sits, right beside the fireplace, reminding me daily of the one who sat in it.

It was my mother's favorite chair.

It also serves as a reminder to me of who I am.

All that my mom experienced is part of my own experience. Who I am is bound up in who she was. The abusive treatment she received affected me. Not because my mom allowed it to, or intended it to, but because the wounds that she carried with her stayed with her for life. Through her those wounds invaded her children's lives in what were sometimes overt ways and sometimes very subtle ways.

I don't think that my mom ever thought that the emotional

wounds she received were injuries that she could expect to be healed. I think that she probably thought that they were just part of her lot in life. That's just the way it was. I think she thought, "The past is past and why would I want to dig up any of that stuff?" Asking God for specific healing for what was wounded in her was probably foreign to her.

My mom very seldom spoke about her past. Some moms today seem to be much more open to exploring the past to find out what might need healing. But still, very few moms are willing to take the time to really deal with areas that need God's healing touch until a crisis hits. Then it becomes relevant.

I hope that what you have read here motivates you to allow God to bring closure and healing before distressing circumstances call attention to your need. If you have realized that you have difficulty accepting who you are, trouble feeling loved, or difficulty standing strong when toughness is called for, it's evident you need God's healing in a part of your life.

God's Plan for Healing

In her article "Redeeming the Legacy of Loss,"[1] Dr. Brenda Hunter tells of the heritage that she received from her mom. Her mom, who was widowed at age twenty-two, did not have the emotional or financial resources to care for two little daughters. As a result, Brenda was left with her grandparents until she was reunited with her mom at age five. She writes of the emotional bond that was severed by separation from her mom—separation that Brenda says was "too early and too long."

Dr. Hunter writes, "With my legacy of loss, it is not surprising that I had difficulty mothering my own babies. Nor is it surprising that I skidded into a full blown depression in my forties when I confronted and reworked my relationship with my mother." But that is not the end of the story. Though her relationship with her own mom was difficult, the Lord healed the wounds in her and in her mom, and blessed her with a wonderful love relationship with her own daughters.

Today Dr. Brenda Hunter has obviously put her "legacy of loss" to purposeful work as she, in the role of therapist, author, and speaker encourages young moms everywhere to be sensitive to the needs of their children.

Whether it be that our moms gave us too much, or left us with places unfilled because of their own woundedness, God has a plan for what was left undone. As we saw in the last chapter, where there was not tenderness, he wants us to experience his tender love. Where there were no limits, he wants us to know his limits and his containment. In order to open ourselves to what God wants to heal in us, I have found that following some guiding steps helps me to stay focused on what he wants to do.

Our usual first reaction to becoming aware of the wounds that we carry around in us is to try to fix them in some way on our own. We jump ahead, wanting relief from whatever it is that makes life so painful. When I realized that I needed help in accepting who I was and in getting the balance between tender and tough I tried to resolve it on my own. I thought I could quickly fix whatever it was in me that made me feel so vulnerable and kept me from standing strong and setting the limits I needed to set. Instead, I had to learn that I needed to go through a process in order to experience healing, God's way.

I don't propose to know how God intends to heal what you bring before him, but these are the steps that I have found to be helpful in my own healing process.

Commitment

First, I began with a commitment to some specific steps that helped me to be patient and see that healing for emotional issues is usually a process. At the same time, I committed myself in prayer to God's loving care and asked him to open my heart to the work of the Holy Spirit. My Heavenly Father is familiar with all my weaknesses and strengths. Because I often err by trusting in my ability to make it on my own, I find it hard to commit to a process that is based solely on God's strength. Often committing ourselves to God's healing process gets at the very core of what it is that we need healing for—our false self-sufficiency. Most of us have difficulty in permitting anyone else to be in charge.

But it is our creator, our Heavenly Father, who designed us uniquely for the role he had for us here on earth who wants to be in charge of our healing.

The psalmist, David, wrote in Psalm 103,

The Lord is merciful and gracious;
he is slow to get angry and full of unfailing love.
He will not constantly accuse us,
nor remain angry forever.
He has not punished us for all our sins,
nor does he deal with us as we deserve.

For his unfailing love toward those who fear him
is as great as the height of the heavens above the earth.
He has removed our rebellious acts
as far away from us as the east is from the west.
The Lord is like a father to his children,
tender and compassionate to those who fear him.
For he understands how weak we are;
he knows we are only dust.

PSALM 103:8-14

We will never completely understand all the ways God has of using the things we experience here on earth to prepare us more for his divine purposes. Nor will we ever understand why some of us have more painful things happen in our lives than others do. But he wants us to make a commitment to the healing process, and to his ability to heal, and then let him fulfill his promise to walk with us through that process.

Awareness

Awareness begins with an understanding of where I am today, and even more importantly, how I got to where I am today—what shaped me. I had to understand that until I faced who I was and the losses I suffered, I would never be able to be the person that I wanted to be. You can't heal a wound by saying it isn't there. Healing always requires that we become aware of what needs healing.

I found that this part of the healing process was difficult but very critical. In looking honestly at what I received, I had to come to terms with the things in my life that might have been at the roots of some of the perfectionistic tendencies I struggle with. I also had to look at who I would be if I gave up those tendencies. I had to face how tenaciously I held on to my identity as being only soft and tender and seldom tough.

I began to realistically look at why I found it difficult to set limits, and I had to become aware of what I had to change in order to be tough when necessary. That led me back to my commitment to allow God to be in charge of my healing and to be also in charge of the consequences of that healing.

Awareness also includes being able to see your relationship with your mom as it really is or was, not the way you wished it could be. It's so easy to distort things because we tend to idealize reality, constantly wishing for things to be different. When we think on the three dimensions of tenderness and admit how we experienced the treatment we received as a child, we can get an honest picture of how things really were and how they probably still are today.

If you still have your mom in your life today you may need to look honestly, as well, at how you really feel when you are around her. Do you walk on eggshells? Are you anxious? Do you shift gears so that you can focus on taking care of mom's needs? Are you frustrated with her? Do you dread her phone call? Do you still feel like a child inside when you are with her? Or are you comfortable and feel as if you have developed a good relationship with her as adult to adult? To be aware means we are honest with ourselves about these questions, too.

Acknowledgment

Once you become aware of what needs to be healed, it's time to talk to someone about it. Acknowledging what you are going through gives concrete reality to it. One of the biggest helps in this healing process is to have someone that you trust with whom you can share the journey. You need a person to talk with, to confess your feelings to, someone who will keep you focused and balanced.

What a blessing it is to find someone with whom you can feel safe enough to share whatever it is that needs to be talked through. I treasure my friendship with my prayer partner, Betty. We have found that there is nothing that we can't discuss with each other. But it took some time to develop the trust necessary to feel that safety—any trusting relationship takes a lot of effort and a big investment of time.

You may find that out of sharing this healing process with another mom, you may develop a safe friendship that lasts well beyond the time it takes to go through it. I trust that developing a deep friendship with another mom will be one of the side benefits you will receive.

It's important to note here that the healing process may not directly involve your mom. You do not need to confront her, or share with her all that you understand about your relationship with her. When I began my own healing process, my mom was no longer living. Many think that when we begin to deal with issues that involve another person they need to involve them in the process. That may come later in the healing process, if Mom is ready and open to it. But it is not a part of your own healing process.

Confession is a biblical word that simply means, "to agree with." James urges us to "confess your sins to each other and pray for each other so that you may be healed" (Jas 5:16). If we are going to accept our reality as true, we need to "agree with" our perception and share it with someone else. Then, if you feel comfortable in doing so, praying together with that person can help you internalize and own that truth.

Grieving the Loss

Grieving over what I lost in my early relationship with my mom was not an easy process. I realized that I not only had to grieve over what I had not received, but I had to grieve over the hidden parts of my mom that I did not get to know.

In grieving, we have to embrace the pain of what we really experienced, without continually negating it by hanging onto the ideal that we have created in our mind. Here we are not just becoming aware of the loss, but also of the pain in the loss.

We will feel great sadness over what has been lost—the ideal of a "good enough" relationship with mom. And we will feel anger at what has been lost. Sadness and anger are the two chief components of genuine grieving.

When we can experience the pain along with the sadness and the anger, we are grieving. The process of grieving takes time and can't be rushed. The deeper our pain, and the more extensive the losses we experienced, the more time we will need to take to grieve. Be careful, you don't want to grieve alone. You need people who will support you in this process, who will encourage you to embrace your genuine feelings and let you know you are loved, and who will tell you when it is time to stop grieving.

What we have lost is what we have longed for: the experience of a tender, warm, and secure relationship with Mom. When we haven't mourned for that loss, we give up any thought of a warm, authentic relationship with anyone else, and we detach ourselves from our feelings, or fill ourselves up with feelings of guilt and shame.

Forgiveness

Grieving over any loss related to the past always leads to the place of forgiveness. After all, what else can we do with the painful parts of our past? Some would answer that question by saying we should confront the person who did the wrong, but that usually leads to more pain and more misunderstanding. Our model for dealing with the issues of the past is God's forgiveness of us. How has he resolved the issue of our sinful past? He has forgiven us. And because we have been forgiven, he expects us to also forgive unilaterally and unconditionally.

Forgiveness is never easy, in part because it goes against the grain of what we consider to be justice. It just doesn't feel right to forgive. Someone must pay. But the meaning of forgiveness in the Bible is that we "cancel a debt" (see Col 2:13-14). We cancel the debt because the other person can't pay. Our mom can't make up for how she raised us. There's nothing she can do now to "pay that debt." So resolution only comes when we cancel the unpayable debt.

George MacDonald said, "It may be infinitely less evil to murder a man than to refuse to forgive him. The former may be the act of a moment of passion: the latter is the heart's choice."[2] Not only is it more evil to not forgive (see Jesus' words in Mt 18:31-35), it is harmful to us physically, emotionally, and spiritually.

Basically, to forgive my mom is to give myself a gift. It means that I have lowered my expectations of what I can receive from my mom to as close to zero as is humanly possible. I release her. I no longer look to her to meet my needs. Makes sense, doesn't it? It makes more sense than continuing to try to get my mom to meet the needs that I have that she has never met in the past.

It's important to understand several things about forgiveness.[3] First, forgiving does not mean we condone what was wrong in our past. What was missing in our growing up years is still missing. When we forgive, we are not saying, "Oh, it's OK that you treated me like that," or, "What you did or didn't do really doesn't matter—it was just fine that way." No, we are canceling the debt when we forgive, not making something that was wrong into something that is OK.

Second, we won't forget what happened to us when we forgive. It would be nice if we could forgive and forget, but that's how God can forgive. We are human; we forgive and remember. In our humanness we need to remember so that we learn how to protect ourselves from further hurt. But forgiveness does mean that we stop rehearsing and nursing the old hurts over and over. We have released our past, and when we remember something painful that we have already forgiven, we need to remember that we have canceled the debt—it is forgiven.

Third, forgiveness does not necessarily mean we have to reconcile. We need to remember that forgiveness is a unilateral process—it only involves me. Reconciliation is a bilateral process that requires that both people enter the forgiving process. I can forgive without the cooperation of the other person if he or she is unrepentant or absent from our lives.

It's interesting to note that this whole healing process we've described so far has not involved Mom. She hasn't been consulted, informed, or included, and she shouldn't be. That means that even if Mom isn't living, or is absent in some other way, we can still work through this healing process that leads to forgiveness.

I talked with a mom the other day who hasn't seen or spoken to her mother in fourteen years. Her mom had gotten involved in the occult. Several times she tried to be around her mom, and found that she just couldn't relate to her. And then when she had her own children, she knew she couldn't have them around her mom. And sadly, her mom doesn't even seem to care. Even though she can't reconcile with her mom, she can forgive her and experience the freedom and healing that comes from forgiving.

The Healing Power of Relationship

God's plan always involves healing within relationships. He wants us to be nurtured by the tender love and gentle spirits of those whose lives touch ours.

We don't usually think of being part of a group as a significant part of our healing process, unless it is a therapy or recovery group. But groups of all kinds can provide the setting for healing if they are nurturing, safe places. My husband and I are part of a group of five couples who have been getting together for the past sixteen years. We go away together for several days twice a year and have learned over the years that this group is a lifeline to each of us. When we are together, we laugh a lot, play a lot, and pray a lot.

The last time we were together I asked some of the women in the group to tell me about their mothers. I found that we were talking about our relationship with our mothers, but that we were also all of a sudden talking about how our mothers' styles had affected us in our present relationships. I realized that we were right then and there in a relationship with each other that gave a clear picture of the issues we each had brought with us into adulthood.

As I was explaining to some in the group what I was writing about, it struck me that the healing power of God had been at work right there under our noses. We realized that as we had cared for each other over the years, God was allowing us to "re-mother" each other. Each one of us brought to that group unmet needs and a different pattern of relating that we developed out of our childhood experiences.

As these women and I have learned to be tender with each others' feelings and to respond to the signals that each of us gives out; as we make ourselves available to each other; and as we accept each other with all our own individual peculiarities, we are modeling to each other God's plan for relationships. We are experiencing remothering in a healthy, wonderful way. We are even learning from each other how to set limits within the context of the tenderness we show each other!

All of us come to relationships with unspoken needs and expectations. Some in our group came with the expectation that every time they got close to someone, they would be rejected. Some of us came expecting to be caregivers, some came as self-sufficient, seemingly needing no one, and some of us came needing care. And this was not just the women who had needs and expectations; the men came, too, with expectations that they placed on the relationships in this group, looking to see if what they expected was going to happen as it had before.

Would it be just as they expected? Would others reject them if they got sensitive and hurt? Would some be offended or maybe turned off when one found the need to expound on a favorite subject? Or would some feel crowded or smothered by so much togetherness?

The wonderful thing about this group of ten is that we have allowed God to work his healing power in our relationships. Each of us in that group has come to realize that whatever we bring has a safe place to be expressed. I wish for every one as safe a place for friendship—a place of "re-mothering" that God uses to fill places that were left unfilled by childhood experiences.

You may not have the opportunity to have such a group, but I urge you to seek out some sort of group. If it becomes a safe place for you, it will be invaluable in your healing process.

When We Face Who We Are

Once I finished the steps outlined here I needed to make sure that I was open to God's working as he made some internal changes within me. As we've already noted, forgiving means giving up the expectations we have for the person we have forgiven. We will always wish that things could have been different, but we are no longer looking for or needing something from Mom. If we still need her to somehow show us that she is accepting us, she still has power over us. Part of what we have grieved and released is the need for anything from her.

Since my mom was not living I had to look at the regrets I still was hanging on to for a relationship that would have been more of a friendship between mother and daughter. When one of my friends tells me that she is taking her mom out to lunch, I still get a twinge of regret, wishing that that could have characterized my relationship with my mom. Then I remember to tell myself that to wish it could have been different is OK—I then use those thoughts as a trigger to remember that I forgave her and the debt is canceled. She doesn't owe me that friendship anymore.

Here are some things you will begin to notice about yourself as you finish this process of healing. To begin with, you will notice that you have a more accurate picture of yourself as the precious treasure God sees you to be. The apostle Paul tells us in Romans 12:3 to, "Be honest in your estimate of yourselves." That means when someone gives you a compliment that is genuine, you can enjoy it because you have a more realistic and appropriate picture of yourself.

Second, you will feel more comfortable setting appropriate boundaries in your relationship with your mom as well as in all of your other important relationships, including those with your kids. It's interesting how healing in our relationship with our moms, helps us be able to handle the other relationships in our life.

Third, others will begin to comment on how much more

responsible you seem—how you are more willing to "own your own stuff." You'll also notice how much more confident you feel about describing to others things that are important to you.

Fourth, you will find that all those things you spent years trying to get from your mom, you are now able to get in the other healthy relationships in your life. Instead of wanting Mom to fill those needs, you are able now to take care of getting your needs met. You can ask others for what you need.

And fifth, you will begin to notice that the experiences you are having don't seem so chaotic as before. Life and all of its experiences don't feel so extreme anymore. It's hard to believe that changes within us can actually seem to change the intensity of what life deals us each day. The Bible describes it as one of the fruits of the Spirit—that of self-control.

When tenderhearted women go through the healing process they find that their tender heart is strengthened and that they all of a sudden have power to be tough when it is called for. The path of healing confirms to tenderhearted moms that their tenderness is their strength, not something that keeps them from standing strong. They begin to trust what their tender heart is saying.

God has already thought through all that we need to experience in order to find healing for the wounds of our past. Sometimes we just wish that he would miraculously heal those wounds quickly, and sometimes he does. But the pattern he seems to choose most often is for us to go through a healing process. That's because there are so many rich lessons we can learn along the way. Remember, as we enter into the process,

God's desire is for healing and wholeness so that we can enjoy all the riches of the abundant life he's promised us as mothers.

We'll look in the next chapter at the practicalities of what we can do when we are called on to get tough, and how to guard our treasure—our tender hearts. We'll look at how God wants to use us in our kids' lives to enable him to create in them a tender spirit.

Thoughts to Consider:
If we courageously face who we are and commit to God's process of healing and forgiveness we will experience the freedom to become the mothers that we really want to be, with a healthy balance between tenderness and toughness. The strength of the tender heart will be evident in us.

What is one thing that you would like to see changed in your relationship with your mom? Or if your mom is not now present in your life, what is one thing that you wish could have been different in your relationship with her?

Which is the hardest part of the healing process for you? Why do you think that is so?

Who are the people that you could have walk alongside you as you go through this healing process?

A Mom's Prayer

Dear Heavenly Father,

Help me to understand that there may be in me wounds that are silent, unseen, and covered that you may want to bring out into your light. I want to become aware of where you want to start the healing process. I am open to the working of your power in me. Will you bless me and keep your hand on me in the process?

In the name of Jesus,
Amen

Chapter Eleven

Meeting the Challenge: Loving Enough to Get Tough

We can't all leave a prestigious background or lots of money to our children, but we can leave them a legacy of love.

NAOMI RHODE

I am reminded of a television commercial that was meant to challenge parents to be more involved in their teenagers' lives in order to prevent drug use. It sums up so well what it is that we tenderhearted moms want to accomplish in getting a balance between tenderness and toughness.

In the commercial four teenagers tell their parents what they had thought of them. One says, "I hated you. I lied and you knew." Another says, "You intruded upon my privacy." Another says, "I thought you were the worst parents in the world." And another says, "I pushed and you pushed back!"

Then there is a long pause and one of the teenagers comes back on the screen and simply says, "Thanks."

They heard the "tough" message and didn't like it one bit at the time. But they must have heard the "tender" message of love as well—for later they could see that the toughness they received was because it was best for them.

It took a lot of courage and confidence for the parents of these teenagers to do what they did.

Tenderhearted Moms Need Confidence

So much of what seems to keep tenderhearted moms from getting the balance between enough tenderness and enough toughness in their relationship with their kids is linked to a lack of confidence. What we have been talking about so far is essentially how to build the confidence that it takes to get tough. Let's review the process:

1. I gain confidence when I begin to learn and appreciate that my tender heart is a precious gift from my Heavenly Father. The more I understand it is a gift, the more I begin to recognize the strength that comes with the tender heart.

2. Confidence comes in knowing that my personality traits are part of my giftedness. Sometimes my personality leans to being too tender and seems to keep me from getting tough. But God gave it to me and it is good. My tenderheartedness is the same trait that makes me compassionate and sensitive to others. God has a special purpose in mind for those he has made especially feeling-oriented. Knowing the bent I have and seeing it as a good quality is a big part of the battle. If I accept the fact that my feeling bent is just as valuable and good as being more objective and thinking, I gain confidence in validating what I feel and learn to listen to my tender heart.

3. When I become aware of how my childhood experiences influenced me as an adult and mother, I begin to see that God's healing and my forgiveness set me free to have con-

fidence to be a better mother in the present. Allowing God to fill places that were left empty in childhood gives me confidence that I can then give out of God's fullness in me instead of trying to give out of an empty cup. Then I can set the limits that will give my kids what they need in the way of structure and containment and also protect my tender heart.

4. Confidence also comes from dwelling on how God models the integration of tenderness and toughness. Trying to change ourselves into a tougher person without understanding God's model is frustrating, and leads to failure and guilt. Trusting God to help me follow his model and finding the balance of tenderness and toughness that is best for me builds my confidence.

5. Confidence comes in knowing that other moms are in this struggle with me. If I feel alone and do not talk to other moms, I can easily get discouraged and get off track. Often I need someone who has walked where I am walking to encourage me. Remember how often it is that God works in relationships to reveal himself. I need to have someone in my life I can trust so that I can say, "OK, I understand all this stuff, but something has come up that has really shaken my confidence. What do I do now?" I will need to have someone remind me of how far I have come, to hear and understand my frustration, and give me some practical steps to do.

Gaining the confidence that God gives through understanding and healing is critical for the tenderhearted mom. It is first.

Now let's look at some things to keep in mind as you continue your journey.

Remember: Tenderness Always Comes First

The most important thing a mom can give is tender care. It will create in her child a reservoir of love. We saw how important tenderness was in giving an infant a chance to form a secure attachment to Mom and how important "gentle hands" are all throughout childhood. We saw how important it is for Mom to be present, to respond lovingly and be appropriately accepting. All these dimensions of tenderness will build that reservoir of love in your child. It will always be there as something for him to draw upon when he needs to.

Tenderhearted moms usually know how to give tender treatment to their young kids. And at times, as we've seen, they may err in being too tender, excluding any toughness. Tenderness is basic and forms the foundation of trust. Without tender love, there is little chance of a child's hearing the tough message later.

Teenagers need all those things that a child needs, but we worry about how we show tender love to our older kids. Of course, tender love has to be given in age-appropriate ways, but a hug or a simple "I love you" is never lost on a teenager. He may seem to rebuff it, but it gets through the filter. Keep giving it, otherwise when it comes time for the toughness, he may not hear you.

When you have adult children, that reservoir of love is still being replenished by those who are in a nurturing relationship with your adult children and yet surprisingly they still need love from Mom. They are hungry for your encouragement, your sensitivity to their needs and for your presence when it is needed. Sometimes moms think they are not needed and cut off relationships with adult children, causing deep hurts. One mom said, "I wish my mom could see that I need her love just as much today, if not more than I needed it when I was little. She does not see it that way. I think that she must think that I would feel babied by her or something if she showed me love now."

I often tell grandmas that their role with their adult kids is to be that of an encourager, a willing, sensitive stand-in if necessary, and a gentle, cautious advisor. How important it is that we are there when we are needed and absent when we are not. Our children who are facing their own stresses in understanding how to be tender and tough as parents themselves need us to continue pouring our love into their reservoir, but in appropriate ways.

Remember: Toughness Is Always Intentional, Never Reactionary

Our toughness is never to be a reaction out of our anger or frustration to something our child has done or not done. When we give tough treatment out of anger or frustration it will go terribly wrong. Our child will never experience it as toughness exercised out of love.

I watched a painful example of reactionary toughness recently. As I sat in my car with the traffic so congested that the light had turned green for the third time and I still had not made it though the intersection, I simply had to relax and wait. It was the day that I intended to write the previous chapter—about what to do once we had learned about all that we had received or had not received from our moms and had asked God for healing of any losses. Writing about mothering has made me so aware of what I see that I have to be careful about making judgments about the quality of care that I might see in a mother-child interaction. I have to remind myself of all the times when I got so worn out and so frustrated that I did not meet the needs of my children. Then I get it in perspective.

But the scene that I saw while sitting there at that corner caused me to cringe. A little boy of about two or three years of age was hopping up and down from off a step in front of the store there at the corner. Mom had apparently told him to stop and he did. Then after hesitating a couple minutes, he turned around and hopped back up on the step. The flash of anger in Mom was startling. She struck out so quickly that it took that little boy by surprise. First she slapped him and then she grabbed a bunch of his hair and pulled it and twisted it. That little boy did not cry out. His mouth was wide open, but he did not cry. An older brother looked on. I wondered if he had seen this before.

Then the mom grabbed the little boy's arm and jerked him off the step, and onto the sidewalk. By now his knees were scraping the cement and then on across the sidewalk she dragged him scraping his bare knees all the way. She roughly jerked him up so that he stood, and then she turned to her companion and continued her conversation as if nothing had happened.

Hopefully we have never treated our children like this mom did, but all moms make mistakes and do things as a reaction which they later regret. Could this mom have possibly thought that she was just "being tough" and that her child really needed that kind of toughness? Maybe this mom was not concerned about what kind of treatment she gave her little son because she was preoccupied with her frustration over her own issues and circumstances. But perhaps she was concerned, but never had the time or energy to give any thought to what her son really needed from her. She needed to understand that toughness only works when it is done by intention, never as a reaction.

What if we find ourselves so stressed that we can't keep from reacting and can't think through the intention of giving the right kind of toughness? There's only one answer: prayer, which is first among four principles moms must apply in order to balance tenderness and toughness.

Principle #1: Bathe Your Shortcomings in Prayer

Many of the things we mothers regret doing have to do with reactions that come out of frustrating interactions with our kids as we try to get them to do what we want them to do. Or they come out of our frustration with other circumstances in our lives and we end up taking it out on our child. Watching the scenario of the mother-child interaction on the corner reminded me of this most important principle that I want to share with you as tenderhearted moms. It concerns the most valuable and powerful force a mother can bring into her relationship with her child. That is to pray about our failures. This is a form of the prayer I have prayed over my years of mothering:

Lord, whenever I fail, whether it be in not being tough enough in setting the limits that my child needs, or failing by reacting out of anger or frustration and saying or doing something I regret, will you correct and repair any hurt that it causes in my child? I ask that where I am weak you will bring someone else into my child's life to fill in the places where I have left gaps in the lives of my children. Will you create in my child an open spirit to receive you and your love?

I have prayed this type of prayer for my kids and myself daily as they grew up. And God has answered that prayer in miraculous ways. My sons have told me of the many times when out of the blue there would be some person or some situation placed in their lives that provided the limits that I was not able to set for them. And as I see two of my sons as fathers, I am amazed at God's work as evident in them as they deal with their kids in tender ways and with a healthier balance of toughness and limits than I had provided for them.

My son, Mike, has a teenage daughter. I remember how impressed I was when I learned that he had told Michelle that when she reached sixteen, that she would not be able to date anyone unless he first met the young man. I wondered how she would take that news. I know that few of her friends had that restriction on dating.

The first couple of times Michelle brought a young man to the house for his "interview," it seemed very awkward for her. She thought that it would be very embarrassing for the boy, but instead, the first one said, "I think that's really good that your dad cares enough about you to make you do this." Michelle had to know that Dad was tough because he loved her so much.

God had "filled in" some of the gaps left by my too tender-hearted approach to mothering. My son had gotten the message from me about how much he was loved, and God had answered my prayer and allowed my son to learn about limits so that he could pass it on to his daughter.

Praying that God will make up for our lack is not a panacea, nor is it meant to relieve us of the responsibility to make changes where we can. But it does relieve us of the burden of trying to remake the past. If we have not been the kind of mom that we wanted to be, we can pray and trust God to make provision for healing any losses our kids may have suffered. God's healing for our own past losses empowers us with a new strength in the present—strength to open our lives to the changes he wants to make in us, and faith to believe for the covering of anything in our kids' pasts.

Principle #2: Make Parenting Your Priority

Which one of us has not yelled at a child who refuses to get dressed for school, or used harsh words when it's time to go somewhere and shoes can't be found. We find ourselves unable to cope with a crying child who does not want to hurry and is obstinately refusing to get into his car seat. We raise our voices, as that seems to be the only way we can get our kids to do anything; we leave the house a mess; we have to rush because we must hurry to get there. Children don't do well when rushed. But we can't seem to change any of it. Our frustration is often fueled because something else has become our priority.

Our children need to see that our relationship with God and

a marriage relationship are priorities, but we also need to let our children know they are next in line. Let them know how important they are by not putting other things ahead of them. One of the problems in our culture today is that many parents seem to want children until they have them, and then they act as if the kids are a bother. Kids of all ages know when we allow other people and commitments to be the pressures that get most of our attention. Children know when they are put last.

In an article by Lori Miller Kase, in *Parents* magazine,[1] she listed some things that will help let your kids know that they are your priority. I've shortened and adapted her list.

1. Make sure your expectations are age-appropriate. This means you have spent time learning what is appropriate to expect from your child at various stages of their growth. Remember, they are children. If your children are teenagers, find out what is right to expect from them, too.

2. Don't take it personally. When children misbehave, remember that children will misbehave. Unless you have created a power struggle with a child to the point that the child is extremely angry with you, their behavior is purposive but not personal. They aren't out to get you.

3. Rely on routines. Even for the spontaneous mom, having routines that can be depended upon gives a child a sense of security. Not everything needs to be a routine, but have some routines your child can count on. Kids who have a routine to follow are less likely to misbehave.

4. Stop repeating yourself. We moms often have the mistaken idea that when our children don't do something we

have asked, we need to say it again, and again, and again. What I found over the years is that repeating myself never worked. If your child hasn't responded, find out why. That takes time, but when parenting is a priority, we can take that time.

5. Help your kids solve their own problems. This also takes time. It's much quicker to just tell them what to do, but in the long run, that will take more time. Slow down enough to ask the right questions that guide your child to the solutions.

6. Address your own stress. Ask what needs to change in your life if you're going to make parenting a priority. Unless you make some of those changes, your stress level is going to increase. Before taking on more commitments remember that the goal is to reduce stress, not increase it.

7. Turn work into play. Be creative. Find ways to redefine tasks, not as heavy burdens but as playful possibilities. Maybe some tasks can never, in themselves, be play. But doing it together can make it into a fun event.

8. Put it into perspective. Childhood doesn't last forever (we hope). These are precious years that can never be repeated. Don't lose sight of the preciousness of what you are doing as a mom. Learn to celebrate the years you have—they go quickly.

Principle #3: The Incredible Five-to-One Concept

What moms don't need is more advice that makes them feel guilty. There are plenty of parenting books available to give guidance in how to set limits and handle discipline, and a lot more on how to love your child. Sometimes a little different twist to things can help.

A few years ago, as I was sitting in a marriage counselor's training workshop, the speaker, Dr. John Gottman began to tell of a principle that he uses extensively in counseling couples. He spoke of it as the "five to one" principle. It went something like this:

It takes five positive behaviors to counteract or override one negative behavior in a relationship.

My husband and I were impressed with that principle and many more that Dr. Gottman was proposing, and we have used them with couples in counseling.

As I thought on this principle, I began to think of it in relationship to mothering. I wondered if it would work the same in the parent-child relationship. I thought, "Aha, here is something that I can teach to moms." Since then I have found that the principle is extremely helpful for moms who are trying to be a great mom and yet who grieve over things that they have done that were not the best.

What we say and do cannot be undone, and we are asking God to take care of the past, but this principle gives moms great hope that they, in spite of their mistakes, can do something in the present—they can pour in the positive and see what difference it makes. I have found this principle has helped moms see that even though they can never mother their children perfectly, they can rest assured that if they would counteract that negative thing that they did with at least five positives, somehow their relationship with their child will be in better repair.

Many moms say that they have a good relationship with their

son or daughter, but once in a while they really lose it and do something that they regret. Using the five to one principle is for moms like them!

But what are the negative things we are talking about? And how big do the positives have to be?

Here are a few of the negative behaviors that we as moms can fall into—behaviors that we never intended to do as a mom. Of course most moms would never think they would abandon, or outright reject their child. These are obviously negatives, but sometimes the behaviors that ultimately lead to these start with interactions that seem benign.

One of the most damaging negative behaviors that takes place in a mother-child relationship is criticism. Genuine toughness is never expressed through criticism. I've talked with a number of moms (and dads) who believe that it is important to use criticism with their child. It is constructive criticism, they say. My husband, as a counselor, teaches that there is no such thing as constructive criticism, as criticism can never be constructive. I have argued with him in the past on that point, but I have since become convinced because I've found that the receiver of the criticism never experiences it as constructive, even when it is invited. Criticism always feels destructive and leads to a lowered sense of self-confidence and worth.

Other destructive behaviors are threats, name-calling and the negating of a child's perception of reality. We could list many examples, but usually a mom knows what it is that she does or says that is negative. As mothers, we are going to do all of these at some time or other. It's part of our being human. But that's what's so wonderful about the five to one principle—we can offset our negative interactions with at least five positives.

The positives include hugs, "I love you" statements, special playtimes, compliments, words of praise, and all the things listed under making parenting a priority. They don't have to be especially big things, but they have to be experienced by your child as tender positives.

Remember the story of the little boy on the street corner? His story had a redeeming factor.

As I continued to watch, the older brother, who was about nine years old or so, now actively entered the scene and took over. He got down on his knees and talked and tried to comfort his little brother who was crying by then. Then I saw it. The older brother gathered that little one in his arms and lifted him up and cradled him in his arms as a tender mother would. Somehow he knew about tenderness and he knew that his little brother needed it right then and there.

Some provision had been made for that little boy—having an older brother who knew about tenderness and who could fill in where there was a void. Maybe brother's "gentle hands" would help create in his little brother the opportunity for a gentle spirit to develop. Maybe he offered some positives that would counteract Mom's negative behavior. I hope so.

Principle #4: The Perception of the Receiver Determines What May Be Too Tender or Too Tough

Remember the four moms mentioned in chapter two who were asking about how strong their no's should be? Let's take another look at their questions to see how what we have been discussing has to do with how tough they needed to be.

First, the mom who had a newborn and was asking about the extreme distress she was experiencing because her husband was insisting that she let their two-week-old son cry himself to sleep. And you already know from the answer I gave her on the spot how I feel about letting a tiny baby cry.

Remember that the primary need for an infant is that Mom be available to her child. It is her presence that provides the secure feelings that allow a baby to learn that the world is a safe place to be. Letting an infant cry himself to sleep is not age-appropriate toughness; it will be experienced as abandonment. Remember what happens if a mom is not available? If a little one is deprived of Mom's presence and her responses, he will decide to do something with his feelings of loneliness. Either he will decide early on that his needs are not valid and shut down his needs or continue trying different ways to get Mom to respond in some way.

So what's the answer for this mom? She needs to see that she and her husband have polarized into tender and tough sides. Mom is taking the tender role and dad has become the tough one. A discussion about what each of them brings to their relationship and to the parenting role in the way of personality and influences from their own childhoods will be helpful. Both Mom and Dad need to read books written from both perspectives—those who advocate toughness for the very young and those who argue that an infant cannot be spoiled at such a young age—so that they can find out where they can agree. One thing is critical—they need to make sure that their baby is building a reservoir of love from which he can draw in order to understand later that limits are because he is loved.

What about the second mom, who wanted to know how to make the decision about whether or not she should allow her now drug-free daughter to come home? Remember that this mom was single and also raising two younger children. She was worried about the influence her older daughter would have on them.

First, let's look at what the teenage daughter needs. This older daughter wants and needs connection to Mom again after being out of the house for a while. But that need appears to be in conflict with the younger children's needs for safety and structure in their home.

So how tough should Mom be? In this case, I feel, very tough. The daughter needs very strict limits, yet needs a chance to repair the relationship with Mom. This mom obviously needs to find a solution that will give her older daughter the connection she needs and yet protect the younger kids. Since the daughter is now drug-free, she can come home. But there must be clear rules that she must agree to before coming home. At the top of the list is to remain drug-free. And this daughter must be willing to do whatever is necessary to assure her mom that she is clean and sober. She also needs to understand the tough part—that if she slips and uses drugs again, she is no longer welcome in the home. Mom needs to express all these limits in the context of her love for her daughter.

What if the daughter doesn't want to do anything to prove she is drug-free? Then it is clear that she is not receiving the "tough" message, and Mom needs to become tougher in what she is saying. The limits need to be reinforced. What if the daughter begins to complain that everything is based on rules and that she is giving up because it's too tough? Then Mom needs to consider several possibilities. Maybe her daughter is only hearing the "tough" message, and Mom isn't expressing the "tender" message. If so, Mom needs to find ways to reassure her daughter of her love for her.

But maybe the daughter is simply trying to avoid accountability in moving home. Mom needs to test this possibility by reassuring her daughter of her love for her, but at the same time underscoring the absolute necessity for limits and accountability. Both the "tender" and "tough" messages need to be emphasized and repeated. Mom can't fear that her daughter might feel rejected by the limits. She would do well to consider what she is bringing to her mothering role from her past that might be serving as a barrier to her getting the message of tender and tough across to her daughter in the right intensity.

The third mom described her difficulty in knowing how to handle her thirty-three-year-old son who was always asking her for money, and who was asking her to continue taking care of his two children. Her son was divorced and had the responsibility of caring for his children. What is she to do? The complexity of her situation is due to the fact that there are grandchildren involved. How can she balance her tenderness and love for her grandchildren with age-appropriate toughness in dealing with her son?

Again, we need to separate the issues. As a grandmother, she truly wants to care for her grandchildren. She has even thought of trying to get custody of them if her son continues to be irresponsible. But she needs to be tough with her son. She knows she has been way too tender. She needs to say something like this to him, "Son, you know I love you. But I can't keep on giving you money. If you ask again, my answer will be 'no.'" And she needs to say this at a time when he is not asking for anything. In other words, she is setting her boundary, and then, of course, when her son next asks for money, she needs to follow through on what she has said. Thirty-three-year-old "children" who are acting irresponsibly need to hear the tough message loud and clear.

Mom also needs to be prepared for her son to somehow use his children to "guilt" her into giving him money. And this is when she will need to have a supportive network of friends who will hold her accountable. She may even need to say to him, "No, I can't give you any money unless I talk with my friends. I'm sorry. I love you, but I have a group of friends who are helping me get through a healing process so that I can get a better balance in my life."

The fourth mom described her overwhelming situation as she struggles to take care of a toddler and a six-month old. She wanted to have fun with them, but found she was always reacting to them in anger. How can she find the balance between gentleness and toughness? My first reaction to her was to look for the roots of her anger. Obviously, she wasn't really angry with her children, because her anger at them didn't even make sense to her. Who was she angry with? Who did she need to set some limits with? My guess was her husband. She said he wasn't much help and wasn't really that involved with the children, and

I suggested to her that she was most likely quite upset with his lack of support. Tears started to come immediately as she agreed.

This mom's task was to begin to deal with the issues between her husband and herself with some "loving toughness." He needed to know about her struggle, and how much she needed his help and support. Nothing was going to change in her relationship with her children until she was able to clear things up with her husband. I saw her a week later and she reported that things had changed dramatically in her relationship with her children, but that she was still working on the talks with her husband. At least temporarily she had felt some relief in just knowing that her problem was with her relationship with her husband and not in her relationship with her children. And she was becoming more aware of what both she and her husband needed to do.

We often struggle with the tougher side of love in our relationships because we all basically fear abandonment. We think if we set limits, the other person will reject us. You can see that in each of these four case studies. If the first mom sets a limit with her husband about letting their child cry, he may get upset with her and reject her. If the mom of the drug-free teenager sets a limit with her daughter, she just might reject everything the mom says and start using drugs again. If the mom of the thirty-three-year-old son refuses to give him money, he just might take his children and leave. And if the mom who needs to confront her husband does so, he just might get mad and leave as well.

In reality, the likelihood of any of these things taking place is remote. But the risk must be faced and limits set and lovingly enforced. Any fear must be faced if it is to be overcome and healed.

The tenderhearted mom who is afraid to risk getting tough will never find the appropriate balance between tender and tough. The mom who takes the risk to get tough will find that her tender heart will be strengthened and that God will provide the courage she needs to get the balance that is best for her and her children. If you follow God's model of love and limits you will open the door for him to bless you and your children abundantly.

"Good enough" mothering always involves risk.

But mothering joys will always outweigh any pain in the risk of getting tough. I guarantee it.

So, will you take the challenge? Will you risk loving enough to get tough?

Thoughts to Consider:
When a tenderhearted mom begins to gain confidence by understanding her giftedness and personality and then allows God to heal her past hurts, she is ready to learn what it is that she needs to change in order to balance the tenderness she gives with the toughness that her child needs. She is ready to meet the challenge of mothering: loving enough to get tough.

What are some of the things that you think still keep you from gaining the confidence you need to really get tough when you see that the situation calls for it?

What do you think of the five to one principle? What are some of the positives that you have used in the past with your children that you might use to counteract a negative in the future?

A Mom's Prayer:

Dear Heavenly Father,

You know how much I want to be the best mom I can be. So will you cover the times when I cannot be tough enough? I trust you for how you are going to use me in my kids' lives and for all that still needs to be done in me. Will you finish the work you have already started in me by healing any residue left in me from my childhood and build in me the strength needed to meet the challenges of mothering? Thank you that I can ask and know that you are willing to bless me and my children beyond anything that I can ask or think.

In the name of Jesus,
Amen

Epilogue

Love is extravagant in the price it is willing to pay, the time it is willing to give ... and the strength it is willing to spend.

JONI EARECKSON TADA

"Just a few more steps and we'll be home," Bessie encouragingly told her younger brother. Bessie and her brothers had walked this trip home hundreds of times, but this day it seemed especially difficult. The sun was hot and made the rails of the train track blistering hot. Once in a while one of the two boys would accidentally step on the hot metal or trip on a sharp stone, and Bessie would hand her book bag to the other brother and reach down and pick up the little one that had a painful foot. She knew that she could not carry him very far because she was not very much bigger than her brothers were, but just for a few feet it would be OK, and she could manage.

Oh, how Bessie loved these little brothers that had come into her life as half-brothers. Her mom had died when she was two years old and these little boys were children born to her stepmother and dad soon after he remarried. Bessie was told, soon after the birth of the first little boy, that it would be her job to watch over this infant and to do most of the caregiving chores that a baby needs to have done. And so she became surrogate mom to that little one and the next, and as they grew she dutifully kept track of them and learned to love them as a mother would.

Now here at ten years old she found that she had the full

responsibility for two young boys ages five and six. This afternoon was not unlike any other as they trudged home from the school that was three miles down the road. Bessie had found that it was shorter to follow the railroad tracks and that the little ones did better with that route. But you see, the really tough part of walking home was the fact that they had to walk home barefoot. They had been told over and over by their dad that if their shoes showed wear too early—earlier than he thought they should—he would give them the "belt" when they got home. So dutifully all three of them carefully took off their shoes before leaving school and tied the laces around the straps of their book bags so that they could get the shoes home with as little wear as possible.

Earlier that week all three of these children had been reminded of what "getting the belt" meant. In a moment of spontaneity, to keep the boys occupied, Bessie had gotten a ladder and set it up, precariously propped, so she could climb to the ceiling of the old barn, which was situated out away from the house. As her brothers watched, giving their important advice every step of the way, for it was their joint project, she climbed up the ladder in order to hang a very heavy rope over some rafters to make a swing for herself and her brothers. How proud they were of the swing with the huge knot in the end.

Little brothers squealing with the fun of the wide sweep the swing made as it carried them back and forth across the barn brought great delight to Bessie. Then it was her turn. She went higher and higher as she pumped the air to make herself swing as far as the rope would go. She had not counted on scraping against the old barn wall, a wall that was rough and happened to have some old nails sticking out right there where her knee touched. She knew she had hurt herself but did not know how badly she had torn the skin on her leg until she got off the swing. Horrified, Bessie and her brothers looked at the gaping hole. What to do now? They knew that in the past when an injury occurred, someone would have to be blamed and punished. The boys quickly ran to the house and secreted some old towels that they felt would not be missed and took them to Bessie. How were they going to hide this injury? They wrapped her leg and mopped up, being careful to put the soiled towels in a remote, little-used trash container behind the barn, hoping that no one would find them for weeks. This would work, they agreed, with Bessie hiding the injury with long pants until they could figure what further they had to do.

Their secret was secure, that is, until they sat at the dinner table that night. Somehow Bessie's dad seemed to be an expert at detecting any little thing that might be hidden from him. Eventually he zeroed in on the boys so intensely that one of them told what had happened. That was it—it was off to the barn for Bessie, the one old enough to have known better. The whipping she got was, as her dad told her, "not because you got hurt, but for hiding it from me."

This is a true story.

Bessie was my mom.

As I look at the worn black rocker sitting in my bedroom, I am reminded that it was probably in that chair that Bessie rocked and sang to each of her five children. I think that it was in that rocker that she made a decision—she would not repeat what her parents had done. She wanted to give her children a tender kind of love. You see, what Bessie did not know is that her children would have loved her just the same had she showed to us some of the parts of her that she kept so carefully hidden. But how was she to know that? She only knew one thing—she would treat her babies with "gentle hands" and build into them a reservoir of love that would last them a lifetime.

For that I greatly love and admire her.

Notes

ONE
The Gift of the Tender Heart

1. *Webster's College Dictionary* (New York: Random House, 1991).
2. Brenda Hunter, *The Power of Mother Love* (Colorado Springs, Colo.: Waterbrook, 1997), 1-2.

THREE
Our Personality Bent May Lean Toward Being Tender

1. The Questionnaire is adapted from the *Myers-Briggs Type Indicator*® as are many of the concepts in this chapter. For more information on the MBTI, contact the Consulting Psychologist Press, 3803 Bayshore Road, Palo Alto, Calif 94303.
2. David Stoop, *Understanding Your Child's Personality* (Wheaton, Ill.: Tyndale House, 1998), 59

FOUR
The Influence of Our Mothering Heritage

1. Quoted in Hunter, 4-5.
2. Henry Cloud and John Townsend, *The Mom Factor* (Grand Rapids, Mich.: Zondervan, 1996), 13.

3. Robert Karen, *Becoming Attached* (New York: Oxford University Press, 1998), 1.
4. Lucy and Dennis Guernsey, *Birthmarks* (Dallas: Word, 1991), 21-22.

FIVE
Our First Lesson in Tenderness

1. Philip D. Eastman, *Are You My Mother?* (New York: Random House, 1960).
2. John Bowlby, *A Secure Base: Clinical Applications of Attachment Theory* (London: Routledge, 1988), 11.
3. Quoted in Karen, 136.
4. From Bowlby's Foreword in Mary Ainsworth, *Infancy in Uganda: Infant Care and the Growth of Love* (Baltimore: Johns Hopkins University Press, l967), v.

EIGHT
We Need Mom's Acceptance With Limits

1. Pia Mellody with Andrea Wells Miller and J. Keith Miller, *Facing Codependence* (New York: Harper Collins, 1989), 7.

NINE
God's Provision for What We Needed

1. Floyd McClung, *The Father Heart of God* (Eugene, Ore.: Harvest House, 1985), 34.
2. Carolyn Stahl Bohler, *God Is Like a Mother Hen* (Westminster: John Knox, 1996).
3. Richard Foster, *Prayer: Finding the Heart's True Home* (New York: HarperCollins, 1992), 84.
4. A.W. Tozer, *The Pursuit of Man* (Camphill, Pa.: Christian Publications, 1950, 1978), 13.

TEN
Making Peace With What We Received

1. Brenda Hunter, "Redeeming the Legacy of Loss," *Focus on the Family*, May 2001, 16.
2. C.S. Lewis, ed., *George MacDonald: An Anthology* (London: Geoffrey Bliss, 1970), 26.
3. See David Stoop, *Real Solutions to Forgiving the Unforgivable* (Ann Arbor, Mich.: Servant, 2001), and *Forgiving Our Parents, Forgiving Ourselves* (Ann Arbor: Servant, 1991).

ELEVEN
Meeting the Challenge

1. Lori Miller Kase, "10 Ways to Be a More Patient Parent," *Parents,* June 2001, 124-131.